TRUSTING THE EYES BEHIND YOU

KAZEMDE AJAMU

"RECLAIMING NARRATIVE, BUILDING LEGACY, EMPOWERING COMMUNITIES"

Copyright © 2025 Kazemde Ajamu
All rights reserved. No part of this book may be reproduced, stored, or transmitted in any form or by any means—electronic, mechanical, photocopying, recording, or otherwise—without the prior written permission of the publisher or author.
Published by:
Black Dot Publishing Company
6984 Main Street
Lithonia, GA 30058
ISBN: 979-8-89269-843-6
First Edition: 2025
10 9 8 7 6 5 4 3 2 1
Printed in the United States of America
Cover Design: 510 Media
Interior Design: Jhavaun Green
For more information, contact Black Dot Publishing Company.

Before you begin this journey of reclaiming your narrative and rebuilding trust, take a moment to center yourself with this affirmation. Let these words ground you in the knowledge that the power to transform lies within you.

AFFIRMATION: I AM

I am duality, as above, So Below, As Within, So Without, As the Universe, So the Soul...
I am the dark and the light; I am East and West; I Am North and South.
I Am my Lower and Higher Self.
I Am Energy.
I Am Connected to All Living Things.
I Am Omnipresent Because I Am Connected, I Am Everywhere all at the same time.
I Am Omnipotent, Through Unifying Energy, I Am All Powerful.
I Am Omniscient, I Know, I Know nothing, but Through the All, we know everything.
Through Collective Action - We Become the All.

I Am the All
As I AM
So Are We
Written by Kazemde Ajamu

At various points in this book, you will be invited to pause and reflect. Use this affirmation as a tool to stay connected with your higher self and the power within you.

Table Of Contents

Introduction: Trusting the Eyes Behind You..10
Explores the central theme of trust as the cornerstone for building relationships, strengthening communities, and shaping a collective legacy.

Chapter 1: The Self Revisited..16
Focuses on rediscovering trust in oneself as the foundation of all relationships, fostering confidence and alignment with purpose.

Chapter 2: Trust in Ourselves:..24
Explores the powerful relationship between self-trust and accountability; emphasizing how personal responsibility strengthens our decisions, relationships, and the community as a whole.

Chapter 3: The Dynamics of Family..34
Examines how trust strengthens families and serves as the foundation for passing wisdom, values, and traditions across generations.

Chapter 4: Community Connectivity..46
Discusses the role of trust in uniting communities and strategies for restoring fractured relationships.

Chapter 5: The Spiritual Dimensions of Trust..56
Explores trust in spiritual principles and unseen forces as sources of resilience and legacy.

Chapter 6: The Need for Community Trust & Healing........................66
. Provides insights into creating a lasting legacy through collective action and shared values.

Chapter 7: Trust and Legacy-Bridging Generations..............................78
Highlights culturally relevant education as a key to reclaiming narratives, fostering identity, and preparing future leaders.

Chapter 8: Igniting Minds: Trusting Education..................88
Discusses how trustworthy leadership inspires collective education and fosters unity within communities.

Chapter 9: Trust and Economic Equity..................100
Explores justice as a means to restore equity and trust in systems shaping our lives.

Chapter 10: Trust in Leadership and Governance..................116
Delves into how collective trust and collaboration can drive meaningful change.

Chapter 11: Trust and Justice..................124
Explores the relationship between justice and trust; emphasizing systemic inequities in the justice system and offering pathways for reform.

Chapter 12: Trust and Shared Leadership..................134
Explores how trust is foundational for shared leadership, collaborative efforts, and community-building.

Chapter 13: Trust and Legacy..................146
Offers strategies for ensuring trust remains central to building a future rooted in shared values and equity.

Chapter 14: Building the Future..................156
Encourages readers to use the principles of trust to empower the next generation.

Conclusion: Foundation For A Brighter Future..................168
Reflects on the transformational power of trust in creating communities and societies where equity and justice flourish.

Sources
A comprehensive list of all the scholarly works, books, articles, and thought leaders referenced throughout the chapters, providing a solid foundation for the ideas presented in the book.

Reflective Questions
Thought-provoking questions at the end of each chapter designed to encourage introspection, helping readers to engage deeply with the material and apply it to their own lives and experiences.

Action Steps
Practical, actionable steps provided at the end of each chapter to guide readers in implementing the concepts and principles discussed, empowering them to make positive changes in their lives and communities.

Foreword

It is a high honor to write the Foreword to Trusting the Eyes Behind You by Kazemde Ajamu. Baba Kazemde is not only a trusted friend, Elder and confidante, he is a source of deep insight, strategy, clarity and wisdom. Baba Kazemde is an absolute treasure to the community. As founder and proprietor of the Black Dot Cultural Center and Bookstore, Baba Kazemde has carved and created sacred space in the historic downtown area of Lithonia, GA for community members to gather for coffee, cultural grounding, book talks, spoken word, music, political organizing and celebrations.

Trusting the Eyes Behind You is a timely book. The lack of trust we see in everyday interactions with community members, romantic relationships, parental relationships and even in business is not by chance. It is an outgrowth of divide and conquer tactics used centuries ago to enslave us and keep us dependent upon oppressors and oppressive practices. The first thing that must be done to conquer a people is to break down bridges of trust and create barriers to trust. This dismantling of trust then brought forth disunity. Lack of trust became a defense mechanism—a response to our collective trauma.

To counter this, Baba Kazemde helped to lead a cultural and political resurgence in the area by facilitating meaningful community gatherings and discussions aimed at actionable outcomes. He was appointed to the Lithonia Housing Authority which further allowed him to advocate on behalf of the people. All of this is the outgrowth of a genuine man of the people with supreme interpersonal communication skills. It was once said of Malcolm X that he could be talking to a person with a doctorate and a drunken man on the street. Both would completely understand him and neither would feel as if he had insulted their intelligence. This is Baba Kazemde. He has a warm, welcoming and natural way of communicating with people from all walks of life. His easy-going energy and infectious sense of humor draws them in. His interpersonal communication is his magnetic superpower and it is clearly evident on the pages of this important book.

Trusting the Eyes Behind You is a very important read. It is practical and easy to read with reflection questions and action steps to help us rebuild our trust muscles. This is an outstanding book to read for book clubs and/or men's and women's groups. Though it is easy to read, it contains deep ideas and lofty ideals. It is just the type of book that can and should spark a resurgence in Black community development, self-determination and trust—and at just the right time, when we need it most.

The recent cultural, political and economic upheavals that have been characterized by anti-Black racial backlash, rising inflation, mass federal government position firings and overall uncertainty should let us know unequivocally that "we all we got." In Trusting the Eyes Behind You, Baba Kazembe takes us on a journey of personal and collective healing that will prepare us for what we must do to make ourselves, our children and our communities whole.

Chike Akua, PhD, Associate Professor
Department of Educational Leadership
Clark Atlanta University
Author, Honoring Our Ancestral Obligations: 7 Steps to
 Black Student Success

INTRO

TRUSTING THE EYES BEHIND YOU

"Trust is the Foundation of everything our relationships, our families, our communities, and even our vision of the future."

Without trust, we are fragmented, unable to build or protect what matters most. But trust isn't just an abstract concept; it's something we practice, live, and rely on every single day.
One of the most profound lessons I've learned about trust came through an exercise I've done in schools, at community gatherings, and with adults during a book release party. It's a simple, physical representation of what trust looks like in action—and it never fails to spark reflection.

The Circle Exercise

Picture this: a room filled with people, diverse in age and perspective, gathered together for a common purpose. I begin the exercise by asking the men to form a circle, standing shoulder to shoulder and facing outward. They are the first layer of protection, their eyes scanning the world outside the circle. Then, I ask the women to stand back-to-back with the men, facing inward, their eyes focused on everything inside the circle. Together, they form a dual boundary of protection, looking both outward and inward.
At the center of this circle sit the elders and the children. The elders represent wisdom and experience, the keepers of the lessons and traditions that guide us forward. The children represent the future—innocent, curious, and dependent on the circle around them for guidance and safety.

Next, I invite a couple into the center of the circle. Standing side by side, they represent union and partnership, a relationship that is both personal and communal. I ask the couple how they see themselves in their union. Without exception, they answer, "side by side." I then stand before them and ask a simple but powerful question: "Can you see behind you without turning your head?" Their answer is always no.
Turning to the men and women in the circle, I ask, "How many people do you see standing before you?" The answer is always two. But then, I ask the couple to stand back-to-back.
Once they're standing back-to-back, I ask each of them again: "Can you see behind you now?" At this point, the answers vary. About 50% of the men say no, and about 40% of the women say no. That's when

I turn to the couple and ask, "If you can't trust the eyes behind you, what are you doing?"

It's in that moment that something shifts. Everyone begins to understand. Trust is not just about seeing—it's about believing that someone else has your back, even when you can't see them.

Finally, I turn back to the entire circle and ask one more question: "Now, how many people do you see when you look at the couple standing back-to-back?" Almost always, the answer is one.

This exercise is a metaphor for trust in ourselves, trust in each other, and trust in the collective. It shows us that no one person can see everything, but together, we can have a 360 degree view of the world. Trusting the eyes behind you means understanding that you are never alone. It means knowing that someone else is watching your back while you watch theirs. And it means accepting the responsibility to protect and uplift one another, building stronger families, communities, and futures in the process.

The Power of Trust and Seeing the Unseen

Trusting the eyes behind you is not just about safety—it's about connection and clarity. It's about moving beyond surface level distractions and opening your eyes to what lies beneath. This concept has a spiritual dimension that cannot be ignored.

In my own journey, I've learned the value of seeing the unseen—looking beyond what's visible to recognize the truth and essence of people and situations. This isn't something that happens automatically; it requires self-reflection, a love lens over your worldview, and a willingness to trust your higher self.

For people of African descent, this concept is deeply rooted in our history. We come from a communal way of life where everyone had a role to play, and the collective was stronger than any individual. But this spiritual understanding has been fractured by centuries of systemic oppression and individualism. Many of us have been taught to see only what's on the surface, to value toughness over sensitivity, and to ignore the wisdom of our inner child.

This book is an exploration of how we can rebuild those circles of trust—starting with ourselves and radiating outward to our families, our communities, and the larger world.

A Call to Reflection

Before we dive deeper, I want to invite you to reflect on your own circle. Close your eyes and picture yourself standing in the middle of a room. Around you are the people who have supported you throughout your life. Who are they? Whose eyes have been watching your back, protecting you when you couldn't protect yourself?

Now, imagine another circle forming around you. This circle is made up of the people who rely on you—your family, your friends, your community. Who are they? How are you showing up for them? Are you someone they can trust to have their back?

This reflection isn't just an exercise—it's a starting point for the journey ahead. Trust is not a one-way street. It is something we give and receive, a cycle that connects us to one another in profound ways.

The Journey Ahead

This book is divided into four parts, each exploring a dimension of trust. We begin with the Self, because trust must start within. If you don't trust yourself—your instincts, your character, your purpose—how can you trust anyone else? From there, we turn to family, examining how trust is built, broken, and healed within the first community we experience. Then we expand outward to explore the role of trust in our broader communities. Finally, we look to society and the systems that shape our lives, asking how trust can transform the world we share.

Throughout this journey, I'll share stories from my own life—stories of questioning, searching, and rediscovering trust. I'll also invite you to reflect on your own journey, asking yourself the same questions I've had to ask:

Who are the eyes behind me?

For whom am I the eyes behind?

How can I build, rebuild, or strengthen the trust that connects me to myself and others?

A Call to Action

This book isn't just about trust—it's about transformation. It's about rediscovering the strength of the collective, even in a world that often feels disconnected. It's about seeing yourself clearly, trusting your instincts, and leaning into the wisdom of those who have come before you.

Trusting the eyes behind you is both a gift and a responsibility. It is a gift to know that someone is watching over you, and it is a responsibility to be that for someone else. Together, these acts of trust create a cycle that connects us all.
Welcome to the journey. Let's begin.

About the Author

Kazemde Ajamu is a visionary leader, community advocate, and lifelong champion for empowerment, education, and cultural pride. His name, Kazemde, meaning "ambassador" in Yoruba, reflects his life's mission: to be a righteous representative who fights for the betterment of his community. With deep roots in advocacy and a commitment to fostering trust and connection, Kazemde has dedicated his life to building spaces of empowerment and enlightenment for African Americans and the broader diaspora.

Kazemde is the founder of the Black Dot Cultural Center and Bookstore, established in 2017 in Lithonia, Georgia. The center has become a hub for community engagement, celebrating Black culture, history, and literature while providing a space for education, dialogue, and connection. Known for its welcoming atmosphere, Black Dot has earned a reputation for excellence, with its coffee shop being named "Best Coffee in Lithonia" by Restaurant Guru and maintaining a high rating from patrons.

In 2023, Kazemde co-founded the Black Men's Advocacy Alliance, a national organization focused on empowering Black men and addressing the unique challenges they face. This initiative amplifies the voices of Black men, fosters systemic change, and creates opportunities for leadership and success.

In 2024, Kazemde expanded this vision by founding the Black Dot Cultural Center & Leadership Academy, a 501(c)3 nonprofit organization dedicated to catering to the needs of the community. The academy provides workshops, events, and leadership programs that promote literacy, personal growth, and collective progress. Through these initiatives, Kazemde continues to build spaces where individuals can connect, learn, and grow.

As the Executive Director of The Urban Politician Alliance, Kazemde has led impactful voter engagement, policy advocacy, and economic empowerment initiatives. His programs, such as the Brick

& Dollar Fund, have supported Black-owned businesses and fostered collective progress. Through his work with the Alliance, Kazemde has helped mobilize communities and shape critical elections in Georgia, advocating for transparency, accountability, and representation.
Kazemde's passion for literacy and education is at the heart of everything he does. He is the founder of Black Dot Publishing Company (formerly Pages to Profit), where he helps independent authors bring their stories to life. He is also the author of Think Black...The Manifesto, a thought-provoking work that challenges readers to explore their cultural identity, purpose, and potential.
Through his podcast, The Urban Politician Show, Kazemde facilitates powerful discussions on social justice, leadership, and culture. His advocacy extends beyond his platforms, actively shaping systems and structures that uplift communities and create opportunities for collective empowerment.
Kazemde believes deeply in the transformational power of love. He often shares the principle that, no matter what your worldview is, you must view it through a lens of love. This perspective informs his work and relationships, creating a foundation of trust, respect, and connection.

Kazemde Ajamu is not only a builder of organizations but also a builder of trust. He inspires others to believe in themselves, connect with their communities, and create lasting legacies of empowerment. His life and work are a testament to the power of love, collaboration, and vision in transforming lives and creating a brighter future for all.

CHAPTER 1

The Self Revisited

"If you have no confidence in self, you are twice defeated in the race of life."
~MARCUS GARVEY

Rediscovering Trust in Yourself

The journey to trust begins within. Before we can trust others, we must first learn to trust ourselves—our instincts, our character, and our purpose. For many of us, self-trust has been eroded over time by the narratives we've been taught about who we are and what we're capable of. These narratives—whether they come from family, society, or our own fears—often shape how we see ourselves and limit what we believe we can achieve. If you don't trust yourself, how can you trust anyone else?

For people of African descent, the question of self-trust is particularly profound. We come from a legacy of brilliance, resilience, and deep spirituality, but generations of oppression have disconnected many of us from this truth. Colonialism and systemic racism have fractured the spiritual and cultural frameworks that once gave us confidence and purpose. These systems imposed false narratives about who we are, convincing many of us to doubt our worth, our potential, and our rightful place in the world.

Reclaiming trust in oneself is not just a personal act—it is a spiritual and communal reclamation. It is an acknowledgment that we are more than the stories told about us. Trusting ourselves means embracing our inherent value and rejecting the lies that were designed to keep us small. It means recognizing that within each of us is a divine spark, a guiding force that has the power to heal, uplift, and transform not just our own lives but the lives of those around us. This chapter is about revisiting the Self—not as an isolated individual, but as a vital part of a greater whole. It's about peeling back the layers of doubt, fear, and distractions to reconnect with the strength, clarity, and divine purpose that has always been within us. When we trust ourselves, we give others permission to do the same. Trust becomes contagious, spreading through families, communities, and entire generations.

A Boy with Questions: Searching for the Truth

As a boy, I loved history. It fascinated me—the stories of the past, the people who shaped the world, and the events that brought us to where we are today. Even when I cut class, I made sure never to miss history. It wasn't just about dates and names for me; it was about understanding the bigger picture and finding my place within it. But even in my favorite subject, I found contradictions. One Sunday after church, I asked my mother a question that had been troubling me. In history class, I had learned about the Middle East and where Israel was on the map—right next to Africa. If Israel was so close to Africa, I wondered, why did every image of Jesus I had ever seen depict him as a white man?

My mother, trying to soothe me, said it didn't matter what race Jesus was. What mattered was his message. But it mattered to me. Even at that young age, I was searching for something deeper—a sense of connection, a truth that made sense in the context of who I was. My question about Jesus wasn't just about religion; it was about identity. I was looking for myself in the stories I was being taught, and I wasn't finding it. That question planted a seed in me—a desire to uncover the truth, to see past the distractions and find a sense of identity that felt real and rooted.

Baba's Lesson: Moving to Your Higher Self

Years later, as a young man, I would sit at the feet of an elder I called Baba, absorbing his wisdom. Baba was a quiet, reflective man whose presence alone commanded attention. When he spoke, he chose his words carefully, and every lesson felt like it carried the weight of generations.

One day, Baba shared a teaching that stayed with me. He told me about the journey from the lower, animalistic self to the higher self. He described the lower self as the part of us driven by survival instincts—fear, anger, greed, and selfishness. "The lower self," he said, "is like a wild animal—reactive, focused only on immediate needs, and easily distracted."

In contrast, the higher self was where true freedom existed. It was the part of us that is connected to love, wisdom, and purpose. "The higher self," Baba explained, "is the version of you that can see the bigger picture. It is rooted in trust: trust in yourself, trust in others, and trust in the divine order of the universe."

Baba used metaphors to bring his lessons to life. "Think of a bird," he said. "The lower self is like a bird on the ground, foraging for food, always looking down, afraid of predators. The higher self is the bird in flight, soaring above the trees, seeing the world from a broader perspective. To rise to your higher self, you must let go of fear and trust your wings."

At the time, this concept felt abstract, even impossible. Seeing the unseen? Moving past my instincts? It sounded good in theory, but how was I supposed to do this in the real world? My life, like so many others, was filled with distractions, survival needs, and daily frustrations. The idea of having a "love lens" over my worldview—seeing the world with compassion and understanding—felt unattainable. I was skeptical, but Baba's calm assurance kept me curious.

Baba emphasized that this journey wasn't about perfection. "The lower self will always be there," he said. "However, the goal is not to let it control you. Each day is an opportunity to choose the higher self over the lower. It's a practice, not a destination."

The Savannah Club: Seeing the Unseen

While traveling to Savannah, I called a friend and asked where I could go to hang out with mature adults. She gave me the name of a club and casually added, "What time are you picking me up?" I wasn't expecting her to invite herself, but we agreed on a time. Later that evening, we arrived at the club and found a seat near the dance floor. At some point, I got up to go to the bar. That's when I noticed her—a beautiful, sexy woman standing alone. My immature mind immediately categorized her as "easy prey." I judged her without knowing her, trapped in my lower self, seeing only the surface.

I returned to my seat, forgetting about her entirely. But later, she got up and began to dance—alone. She moved with a grace and freedom that was captivating. As the music took over her body, it was as though she entered a zone where nothing else existed. She was unaware of anyone watching, entirely in her own world.

The more I watched her, the less I saw her as a sex object. Slowly, her beautiful spirit came into focus. I began to see the unseen. It was then that I realized most of what we perceive are distractions, illusions designed to keep us trapped in our lower selves. This woman wasn't just dancing—she was embodying her higher self.

That night in Savannah marked a shift in my life. I began to trust myself and my ability to see beyond the surface, to recognize the divine essence in others and in myself.

Reflection on the Child Within

As I continued my journey, I developed a practice that has shaped the way I see people. When I meet someone, I look for the child within them. We all show it at times—a glimpse of the innocence, curiosity, and authenticity that reveal who we truly are. That inner child is the holder of our true selves, the guardian of our divine purpose.

But life has a way of burying that child. Circumstances, societal expectations, and survival strategies mold us into people we think we have to be. We mistake those identities for truth, forgetting that our real truth lies in the child within us. The child within holds the key to our joy, our creativity, and our ability to connect with others on a genuine level. Yet, over time, many of us lose touch with this essential part of ourselves.

This practice of seeing the child within has changed the way I view others and how I move through the world. When I see someone acting out of anger, fear, or pain, I remind myself that it's often their wounded child crying out. Instead of reacting with judgment, I strive to respond with compassion, seeking to understand the unspoken story behind their actions.

Reconnecting with that inner child is not just an act of self-healing—it's an act of resistance against a world that often seeks to dehumanize us. It is reclaiming a part of ourselves that society has tried to strip away. When we embrace the child within, we unlock the ability to live more authentically, to connect more deeply, and to trust ourselves without hesitation.

The Role of Self-Honesty

You cannot begin to trust yourself if you are not honest with yourself. Self-reflection is not just a skill; it's a necessity. Honesty with oneself is the foundation of self-awareness and personal growth. It allows us to take responsibility for our actions, our choices, and the roles we play in the dynamics of our relationships. Without this honesty, we risk falling into patterns of blame and denial, which only serve to deepen our disconnection from ourselves and others.
In every situation, particularly when confronted with conflict, I ask myself: What role did I play in this dysfunction? It's not always easy to face the answers. Sometimes, the truth grounds me in clarity. It allows me to see a path forward for reconciliation. Other times, I

realize I had unrealistic expectations of someone. I knew they weren't capable of delivering what I expected, so why am I angry? In those moments, I see how I created the conflict, and the anger dissipates. This kind of honesty is liberating. It removes the illusions and distractions that keep us trapped in cycles of blame and frustration. Trusting yourself means being willing to see the truth—even when it's uncomfortable. It also means forgiving yourself when you recognize your mistakes. Self-honesty is not about self-punishment; it's about growth. It's about learning to align your actions with your values and intentions.

One of the most powerful outcomes of self-honesty is the ability to set realistic expectations. Too often, we place expectations on others that they are simply not equipped to meet. We expect people to love us in ways they were never taught to love themselves. We expect understanding from those who have never been understood. And when they fall short, we feel betrayed.

But when we're honest with ourselves, we can see the truth of who they are and adjust our expectations accordingly. This isn't about lowering your standards—it's about grounding them in reality. Self-honesty doesn't mean you accept mistreatment or ignore red flags. It means you approach every situation with clarity and compassion, including compassion for yourself.

Conclusion: The Transformative Power of Self-Trust

Self-trust is the foundation upon which all other forms of trust are built. Without it, our relationships with others, our communities, and even our sense of purpose become shaky and uncertain. Reconnecting with yourself—your inner child, your higher self, and your honest truths—is an act of liberation. It allows you to move through life with confidence, clarity, and an open heart.

The journey to self-trust is not a straight line. It is a winding path filled with moments of doubt, reflection, and growth. But each step forward strengthens your foundation, making you more resilient, more compassionate, and more aligned with your true purpose. When we trust ourselves, we also inspire trust in others. Our actions, grounded in authenticity and integrity, create ripples that extend beyond us, shaping our families, our communities, and future generations. Trusting yourself is not just a personal act—it is a legacy you leave behind, a testament to the power of believing in the divine spark within.

REFLECTION QUESTIONS

What experiences in your life have shaped your self-trust?

How has questioning established narratives led you to rediscover your truth?

What steps can you take today to align more closely with your higher self?

Action Steps

Explore Your Beliefs: Identify one narrative about yourself you've accepted but have never questioned. Reflect on whether it aligns with your truth.

Embrace Daily Practices: Set aside time each day to reconnect with your higher self through meditation, prayer, or journaling.

Share Your Story: Begin a conversation with someone you trust about a time when you doubted yourself and what you learned from it.

Notes

CHAPTER 2

Trust In Ourselves

"Accountability is the glue that ties commitment to results."

~Bob Proctor

Introduction: The Power of Accountability

Self-trust is not a static condition; it is an evolving practice of making conscious, intentional choices. One of the strongest foundations of self-trust is accountability—our ability to take responsibility for our actions, decisions, and the outcomes they create. To trust ourselves fully, we must hold ourselves accountable for both our triumphs and our failures. Accountability isn't just about acknowledging mistakes—it's about owning the power to course-correct, learn, and grow.

This chapter is about understanding the symbiotic relationship between trust and accountability. Trust begins with the belief that we can make sound decisions, but it deepens when we hold ourselves accountable for the results of those decisions. Accountability is not only about being answerable to others—it is about being answerable to ourselves, staying true to our values, and upholding the promises we make, both to ourselves and to others.

In the context of African-descended communities, self-trust and accountability have long been central to survival, resilience, and growth. Historically, our families, communities, and ancestors understood the importance of personal responsibility as a means of preserving dignity and agency in a world designed to strip those very qualities from us. In times of oppression and adversity, trust in ourselves and our ability to be accountable to each other became critical tools of survival.

Reclaiming self-trust and embracing accountability is therefore an act of resistance. It is a return to self-determination, a decision to no longer allow external circumstances, societal expectations, or past trauma to dictate our futures. By trusting ourselves and holding ourselves accountable, we reclaim control over our lives and ensure that the decisions we make are aligned with our higher purpose.

Dr. Na'im Akbar on Self-Accountability and Liberation

Dr. Na'im Akbar, a prominent African American psychologist, emphasizes the importance of self-empowerment and responsibility as integral components of personal and community healing. In his book Breaking the Chains of Psychological Slavery, Dr. Akbar explores the ways in which African Americans have been conditioned by a history of oppression, but also stresses the importance of reclaiming the self through accountability. He writes: "True liberation begins when we take full responsibility for the state of our own minds. Accountability is not only about accepting the consequences of our actions but reclaiming our agency, our capacity to shape the future."

Dr. Akbar's words underscore the relationship between self-trust and the ability to hold ourselves accountable. For African Americans, this means rejecting external narratives of inferiority and replacing them with an empowered understanding of who we truly are—an understanding that starts with self-accountability.
As Dr. Akbar highlights, accountability is an active, intentional process that requires us to not only acknowledge the external influences that have shaped us but to take responsibility for our own growth and future. It is about rejecting the limitations imposed by a history of oppression and replacing them with the agency to create new, more empowering narratives about who we are and what we can achieve. Incorporating this perspective into the practice of self-trust means understanding that accountability is not about perfection, but about the continued effort to reclaim our power. It means trusting ourselves enough to take ownership of both our progress and setbacks, knowing that both are part of the journey toward healing and growth.

Accountability in Motion: Building Trust Through Integrity

When we are accountable to ourselves, the effects are far-reaching. Our actions don't just shape our own growth; they influence those around us—family, friends, colleagues, and even strangers. Accountability is not a solitary practice; it is a relational one. It forms the foundation of the trust we build in our lives and how we contribute to a culture of mutual respect, understanding, and personal growth.

Personal integrity is the root of accountability. When we consistently hold ourselves to the highest standards, we demonstrate the kind of responsibility that others can rely on. This practice has a ripple effect—our commitment to being truthful, responsible, and self-aware encourages others to do the same. It's through our example that we cultivate an environment where trust is not only possible but also actively nurtured.

However, accountability requires courage. It's not always easy, nor is it always comfortable. True accountability demands that we face our own flaws and shortcomings. It asks us to look in the mirror, acknowledge where we've fallen short, and take ownership of our actions without excuses. Accountability challenges us to make difficult choices, often stepping outside of our comfort zones and facing discomfort head-on.

But it is in these moments of discomfort that real growth occurs. Through accountability, we learn to navigate life's complexities with a clearer sense of purpose, resilience, and inner peace. When we hold ourselves accountable, we empower ourselves to rise above the obstacles that might otherwise deter us. It is not about avoiding the hard choices but embracing them as opportunities for self-discovery and transformation.

At the heart of accountability is self-reflection. This is not a one-time practice but a continuous, active process. To live in alignment with our highest values, we must periodically check in with ourselves. We must ask the difficult questions: "Am I living according to the standards I've set for myself? Am I acting in a way that honors my values and my commitments?"

Answering these questions honestly forms the bedrock of trust. Trust is built on the integrity of our actions, and it is through our accountability to ourselves that we establish trust with others. When we can look at ourselves without flinching, knowing we've acted in alignment with our truest selves, we lay the foundation for stronger relationships and a greater sense of peace.

Accountability, therefore, is not just about our actions—it is about ensuring that we are true to ourselves. This act of self-honesty builds the resilience needed to withstand the inevitable challenges and tests that life will present. It ensures that when we fall, we can rise again—stronger, more grounded, and with a renewed sense of purpose.

Through this kind of accountability, we create a legacy of integrity. It's not just about correcting mistakes; it's about forging a path forward with conviction and authenticity. By holding ourselves accountable, we become active participants in our own lives and in the communities we inhabit. This commitment to accountability ripples outward, creating a culture of trust and responsibility that extends far beyond our individual selves.

The Power of Self-Accountability in Healing and Growth

Personal growth and healing are fundamentally linked to self-accountability. When we take full responsibility for our lives and our decisions, we open the door to transformation. Accountability is not about perfection; it is about progress. It is about showing up for ourselves every day, taking ownership of our actions, and being willing to make the necessary changes when things don't align with our true purpose.

Through accountability, we also begin to heal from the past. Many of us carry the weight of generational trauma, societal pressures, and personal disappointments. We may feel that we are trapped in patterns of behavior that no longer serve us. But when we accept responsibility for our role in perpetuating those patterns, we break free. We give ourselves permission to rewrite our story and embrace the freedom that comes with taking charge of our own lives.

The journey to self-trust is a continual process of accountability. It requires us to stay committed to our own growth and healing, to trust our inner voice, and to hold ourselves accountable for our actions. In doing so, we begin to see ourselves as active participants in our own lives—no longer passive observers but empowered agents of change.

My Story of Accountability:
The Bar Tab and the Woman at the Club

One personal story that illustrates the importance of self-accountability occurred during an evening out at a club. As I stood at the bar about to pay my tab, I noticed someone standing behind me. I turned around to find an attractive woman smiling at me, who mentioned that she had seen me at the club a few weeks ago and wanted the opportunity to speak with me. Instead of just paying my tab and leaving, I chose to buy two drinks for us both, and we sat down to engage in a captivating conversation. The chemistry between us was undeniable.

After some time, she asked if I was involved with someone. I told her I was seeing someone but it hadn't reached the level of commitment yet. She responded by suggesting we move forward. In that moment, I paused, reflecting on the situation and replied, "You know, Sister, there's obviously great chemistry between us, but we need to take the time to figure out what the nature of this chemistry is. Is it that we are supposed to be good friends, acquaintances, or lovers?

What if this is just a fleeting moment in time?"

This story demonstrates the importance of taking a step back to understand the deeper nature of our interactions before rushing in. Too often, we fail to pause and reflect on our intentions, rushing forward based on chemistry or impulse. By choosing to reflect and be accountable to myself in that moment, I was able to make a decision that was grounded in intentionality and self-awareness. This is how true accountability works: by recognizing our power to decide, to define relationships, and to trust ourselves in the process.

This moment was more than just a brief encounter; it was a lesson in accountability and self-trust. By taking the time to question the nature of the relationship, I was able to make a decision that honored my values, my relationships, and my own boundaries. It's an example of how accountability to ourselves creates clarity and builds trust, not just within ourselves, but also with others.

Conclusion:
Trust and Accountability as Catalysts for Personal and Family Transformation

Self-trust and accountability are not just abstract ideals—they are the very bedrock of personal transformation and community resilience. As we navigate the journey of life, we must constantly refine our relationship with ourselves and others through accountability. This relationship is not a static achievement but a continuous process—one that evolves with each decision, each lesson, and each act of self-reflection.

To trust ourselves fully means we must embrace accountability—not just in moments of success but especially in moments of failure. It means owning our actions, learning from them, and adjusting our course when necessary. Accountability is not just about external judgment or validation; it is about being answerable to ourselves, aligning our actions with our values, and upholding the promises we make—both to ourselves and to those we love.

The act of holding ourselves accountable begins with the quiet, internal commitment to be better—to act with purpose and integrity. As we do this, we begin to see the profound impact our personal choices have on those around us. The act of being accountable is not just for our own growth; it sends a message to those in our lives, particularly our families, that trust is something we actively cultivate and honor. When we practice self-accountability, we set an example. Our families, our communities, and the relationships we nurture are all influenced by our actions. In this way, accountability becomes a powerful tool for collective transformation. It shapes the trust we build with our loved ones and extends outward into the communities we serve.

However, accountability is not without its challenges. It requires us to confront our imperfections, acknowledge where we've fallen short, and embrace discomfort as a necessary step in our growth. But it is through these moments of discomfort that we experience our most profound lessons. Accountability is not about shame or self-punishment; it is about embracing our agency, stepping into our power, and taking responsibility for the outcomes we create. The journey to reclaiming trust begins within, but it is not a solitary endeavor. As we embrace self-accountability, we begin to see its ripple effects—not just in our own lives but in the lives of those we love. When we take ownership of our actions and strive to live with integrity, we create a space for others to do the same. This process builds a foundation of trust that stretches beyond the individual, fortifying relationships, families, and communities.

As we continue on this path of self-trust and accountability, we see the interconnectedness between our individual growth and the growth of those around us. By committing to be better versions of ourselves, we open the door to deeper connection, greater understanding, and lasting impact. This journey is one of personal healing and transformation, but it is also one of communal empowerment—each step we take toward self-accountability has the potential to transform the world around us.

Now that we have explored the importance of accountability in building self-trust and empowering ourselves, we can begin to look outward. In the next chapter, we'll dive into Chapter 3: The Dynamics of Family Trust, where we'll explore how the principles of self-trust and accountability extend to our families. Family, as the first place where we experience trust, is where we begin to see the ripple effects of our individual growth. We'll examine how trust is cultivated within families, how it can be nurtured, tested, and even rebuilt after it's been broken, and the essential role each family member plays in strengthening this foundational unit. Trusting ourselves lays the groundwork for trusting each other—and when we begin to trust within our families, we start to build communities that are resilient, cohesive, and powerful.

REFLECTION QUESTIONS

How have you practiced accountability in your own life, especially in moments of personal or family challenges?

What steps can you take today to become more accountable to yourself and others in your community?

How do you navigate the discomfort of accountability, especially when it reveals areas for growth?

What role does accountability play in healing generational trauma within your family or community?

Action Steps

Reflect on a recent decision you made and identify how accountability played a role in the outcome.

Commit to taking responsibility for one area of your life where you've been avoiding accountability.

Share a story of self-accountability with someone you trust, and encourage them to do the same.

Notes

CHAPTER 3

THE DYNAMICS OF THE FAMILY TRUST

"A family is like a forest: when you are outside, it is dense; when you are inside, you see that each tree has its place."

— African Proverb

The Family Circle-Family is where we first experience trust—or the lack of it. It is the circle we are born into, the foundation that nurtures us, shapes us, and teaches us how to see the world. Ideally, trust flows freely within this circle. Parents guide and protect their children. They rely on their parents' wisdom, and siblings stand together as allies. Yet family can also be where trust is broken most deeply, leaving scars that ripple outward into every relationship we form.

For people of African descent, family has historically been a cornerstone of resilience. Enslavement, Jim Crow laws, and systemic racism sought to dismantle Black families, yet they persisted, often becoming the bedrock of survival and strength. Grandparents raised grandchildren, fictive kin stepped in where blood relatives were lost, and communities operated as extended families. In this context, family was not merely a biological unit—it was a cultural and spiritual sanctuary.

However, the same historical forces that made family indispensable also introduced fractures. Families were torn apart by systemic violence, economic exploitation, and mass incarceration. This legacy has left many families grappling with trust—how to form it, sustain it, and rebuild it when it has been broken. One of the most insidious contributors to family distrust is the presence of family secrets. These hidden truths—whether about finances, relationships, health issues, or past traumas—create barriers between family members, breeding suspicion, shame, and resentment. Secrets often become invisible walls that prevent families from achieving true closeness and trust. Left unaddressed, they poison relationships for generations.

This chapter explores the dynamics of family trust—how it is formed, how it is tested, and how it can be rebuilt. It examines the family as a circle within the larger community and reflects on the role each member plays in holding it together.

The Circle of Protection

In the circle exercise I often lead, elders and children sit at the center, surrounded by adults who form a protective barrier. This configuration reflects the ideal family dynamic. Elders, with their wisdom and experience, are the anchors of the family, guiding and advising from a place of love. Children, representing the future, are nurtured and protected as they grow into their potential. The adults, standing shoulder to shoulder, face outward, shielding the family from external harm while also supporting those within.

The exercise is powerful because it reveals not only the ideal but also the gaps. Participants often feel the weight of their roles. Adults realize how much the strength of the circle depends on their solidarity. Elders see the gratitude and reliance placed upon their wisdom. Children feel the safety of being encircled. But when the circle breaks, the vulnerabilities become clear. Children feel exposed, elders lose their grounding, and adults experience the strain of standing alone.

What happens when this circle is broken? When parents are absent, elders are silenced, or the protective barrier weakens, leaving children vulnerable to the harsh realities of the outside world? The breakdown of trust within the family mirrors the breakdown of communal trust that once held our communities together.

The exercise also reveals a truth: the family circle isn't static—it is dynamic. Members move in and out of roles as life progresses. Children grow into adults. Adults become elders, and the cycle continues. Trust is what allows these transitions to happen smoothly. Without trust, the circle falters, and the family's ability to withstand external pressures diminishes.

The Harm of Family Secrets

Family secrets often begin with good intentions. Parents may hide financial struggles to shield their children from worry, or past traumas may be buried to avoid reliving painful memories. However, these secrets create a false sense of reality within the family, distorting communication and making it difficult for members to trust one another fully.

The harm of family secrets extends far beyond the immediate circumstances. They breed mistrust, as family members sense that something is being withheld but are left to speculate or make assumptions. These unspoken truths manifest as anxiety, tension, or estrangement, as the emotional weight of what is unsaid overshadows relationships.

Children are particularly affected by family secrets. Growing up with an incomplete narrative of their family, they may develop insecurities or a fear of asking questions. This lack of transparency can lead to a breakdown in trust that persists into adulthood, making it harder for them to form open and honest relationships in their own lives.

In some cases, family secrets become generational burdens. A hidden truth—such as an unacknowledged child, a history of addiction, or undisclosed financial debts—can resurface in the next generation with compounded consequences. The effort to keep the secret intact drains emotional energy that could be used to strengthen family bonds.

Healing Through Transparency

The first step to addressing the harm of family secrets is a commitment to transparency. Families must create safe spaces for open communication, where difficult truths can be shared without fear of judgment or retribution. This process requires courage, as it often means revisiting painful experiences or admitting past mistakes. However, it is only through this honesty that trust can begin to be rebuilt.

When addressing family secrets, it's essential to approach the conversation with empathy. The goal is not to assign blame but to seek understanding. Why was the secret kept? What impact has it had on the family? By focusing on these questions, families can begin to unpack the root causes of the secrecy and work toward healing. Forgiveness also plays a critical role in this process. Family members who feel betrayed by a secret may need time to process their emotions and come to terms with what they've learned. Forgiveness doesn't mean forgetting or excusing the harm caused—it means choosing to move forward with the intention of rebuilding trust.

In some cases, seeking the guidance of a neutral third party, such as a therapist or counselor, can help facilitate these difficult conversations. A trained professional can provide tools and strategies for navigating sensitive topics, ensuring that all voices are heard and respected.

Robin's Role: Rebuilding Confidence Through Trust

My journey with family trust has been shaped by pivotal lessons, particularly during one of the most challenging periods of my life. After serving time in a federal prison camp, I returned home with my confidence shattered and my future uncertain. My wife, Robin, had stood strong during my absence, but I struggled to trust myself, and that lack of trust spilled into my relationships, including our marriage.

Finding work after my release felt impossible. Each interview ended the same way—the energy shifted when I disclosed my felony record. Each rejection felt like a blow, eroding what little confidence I had left. In response, I turned to hustles, selling copier supplies, incense, and T-shirts, but nothing seemed to stick. Robin, however, refused to let me lose sight of my potential. She pushed me relentlessly, challenging me to stop masking my pain with distractions and to focus on rebuilding.

At the time, her critiques felt harsh. I interpreted them as attacks on my character and began to question her support. Instead of discussing what was bothering me, I would shut her out. When things felt overwhelming or her words stung, I avoided the conversation altogether, retreating into my own silence. But this didn't solve anything. If anything, it deepened the disconnect. I felt unsupported, and I resented her constant critique, often thinking, "She doesn't have my back. I'm done."

But deep down, something told me to stay. One day, standing in our dining room, I decided to draw a line—not against her, but for myself. I told her I was committed to building something real, starting with my T-shirt line promoting the message Think Black. That moment was a turning point—not just for our relationship but for my own sense of self.

Robin saw the seriousness in my determination, and her perspective shifted. What once felt like criticism became a reflection of her belief in me. She wasn't trying to tear me down—she was trying to push me toward the man she knew I could become. Over time, we began to trust each other more deeply. I saw her critiques for what they truly were: acts of love and accountability. She saw my potential long before I could, and that trust became the foundation for not just our marriage but our family.

Learning the Art of Communicating With Trust

One of the most transformational lessons I've learned in our journey together was the importance of how and when to communicate—especially in moments of emotional tension. Early in our relationship, I would let things fester. Instead of speaking up about what was bothering me, I would retreat, shutting Robin out completely. My silence was my shield, but it also became a barrier to trust and connection.

Over time, I realized that this wasn't sustainable. Avoidance wasn't solving the problem; it was deepening the divide. Robin's critiques, though hard to hear, were rooted in her belief in my potential. But if I couldn't express how her words made me feel—or worse, if I reacted out of anger—how could she know how to adjust?

The turning point came when I began to understand the value of pausing. Instead of responding in the heat of the moment, I learned to stop, control my emotions, and reflect. I asked myself: "What am I feeling? Why does this bother me? How can I communicate this in a way that Robin can hear, rather than react defensively?" That shift changed everything. I started to approach difficult conversations with intention, thinking through my words and ensuring that they reflected what I truly wanted to express. In those moments of reflection, I realized that speaking out of anger or frustration rarely achieved what I wanted. If anything, it pushed Robin further away. But when I spoke calmly and clearly, she could receive my words. This wasn't easy to master—it took time, patience, and plenty of trial and error. There were moments when I slipped, when my emotions got the better of me. But I kept coming back to the principle of trust: trusting myself to communicate with care, trusting Robin to receive my words with love, and trusting that our relationship was strong enough to handle even the toughest conversations.
By learning to communicate in this way, I not only strengthened our marriage but also grew as a person. I began to see how powerful it was to pause, reflect, and choose my words carefully—not just with Robin, but in all my relationships.

<u>Trusting the Eyes Behind Me</u>

Robin's belief in me taught me one of the most profound lessons about trust: it isn't always comfortable. In the past, I had seen her challenges as attempts to undermine me, but they were really her way of helping me navigate forward. Her ability to see what I couldn't—to recognize my potential when I was too consumed by doubt—helped me understand the value of trusting the eyes behind me.

Trusting someone when you feel vulnerable is one of the hardest things to do, especially when your confidence has been shaken. Robin taught me that trust isn't about agreement—it's about believing in someone's intentions, even when their approach feels uncomfortable. Her guidance forced me to confront my insecurities and move past them, to embrace the idea that growth often comes from the very critiques we resist the most.

That shift in perspective transformed how I approached all my relationships. I began to surround myself with people who challenged me, who held me accountable, and who saw the potential I couldn't yet see in myself. Trusting the eyes behind me became a principle I carried into every aspect of my life, starting with Robin.

The Role of Elders: Wisdom and Guidance

In every family, elders play a critical role. They are the keepers of stories, the bearers of wisdom, and the ones who can see beyond the immediate struggles to the bigger picture. Elders like Baba remind us that family trust isn't just about protecting the present—it's about connecting to the past and building a bridge to the future. Baba once told me, "A family without its elders is like a ship without a compass." His wisdom guided me through my darkest moments, reminding me to look beyond the immediate pain to see the lessons it held. Elders like him have a way of seeing through the fog of our emotions, offering clarity and perspective that we often lack in the moment.

"A Village without Elders is like a well without water" ~African Proverbs

Elders are not only storytellers but also cultural archivists. They hold the memories of past generations, the traditions that have been passed down, and the lessons learned through hardship. By listening to their stories, we gain insight into how our ancestors navigated challenges that may seem insurmountable to us today. Their experiences remind us that resilience is in our DNA.

Yet, the role of elders has been diminished in many modern families. Their voices are often dismissed as outdated, and their wisdom is ignored in favor of instant gratification. In an age dominated by technology, the wisdom of an elder may seem less accessible than a quick internet search, but no digital resource can replicate the depth and nuance of lived experience.

"What the youth see while standing on their toes, the Elders see while sitting down." ~African Proverbs

Rebuilding family trust requires us to reclaim the value of our elders. It means creating spaces where their voices are heard and their contributions are honored. It means teaching younger generations to respect their guidance and to see elders not as relics of the past but as vital resources for the present and future. When we reconnect with our elders, we not only strengthen the family but also tap into a wellspring of cultural and spiritual wealth.

The Inner Child and the Family Dynamic

As I've grown older, I've come to believe that one of the most important roles of the family is to nurture the inner child in each of its members. That inner child represents our true self—the part of us that knows our divine purpose. But too often, family dynamics suppress that child. Parents, trying to protect their children, may unintentionally project their own fears and limitations onto them. Siblings, caught in competition, may stifle each other's growth. The inner child is both fragile and resilient. It holds our creativity, curiosity, and capacity for joy. But when it's stifled, it retreats, leaving us disconnected from ourselves and others. Families that fail to nurture the inner child often produce adults who carry unresolved pain, mistrust, and a sense of inadequacy.

I've witnessed how generational trauma can silence the inner child. Parents, shaped by their own unhealed wounds, may impose unrealistic expectations on their children or criticize them in ways that stifle their confidence. These patterns create a cycle of mistrust and emotional suppression that can span generations.
But families that commit to seeing each other fully—beyond the surface behaviors and roles—can break this cycle. Nurturing the inner child requires patience, compassion, and a willingness to embrace vulnerability. It means recognizing when someone's anger or withdrawal is a cry for help and responding with understanding rather than judgment.

When families create an environment where the inner child feels safe, they unlock a profound capacity for healing and growth. This process doesn't just benefit the individual—it strengthens the entire family. A healed inner child often becomes a more present, loving, and trustworthy adult, capable of contributing to the family's collective well-being.

Healing the inner child within the family dynamic is an act of generational repair. When one member begins to heal, it creates a ripple effect, inspiring others to confront their own wounds. This collective healing process builds trust, deepens connections, and lays the foundation for a stronger, more resilient family.

The Challenges of Black Men and Vulnerability

For Black men, family trust often comes with unique challenges. Many of us are taught that vulnerability is a weakness, that strength is about toughness and stoicism. We learn to suppress our emotions, masking our pain and fear until it erupts in destructive ways.

This conditioning doesn't just hurt us—it hurts our families. When we show up as unfeeling, emotionally unavailable robots, we create barriers to intimacy and trust. Our spouses, children, and siblings often feel disconnected from us, unable to see past the armor we've been taught to wear.

I've had to unlearn these lessons about masculinity. For years, I believed that being strong meant hiding my emotions, but I've come to understand that true strength lies in vulnerability. It takes courage to express how you feel, to admit when you're afraid, and to lean on the people who love you. In doing so, you allow them to trust you more deeply, knowing that you're fully present and authentic.

This shift isn't easy, especially when societal pressures reinforce old patterns. But it's necessary. Black men have the power to transform their families by embracing vulnerability, showing love openly, and trusting that their emotional honesty will be met with understanding and support.

Rebuilding the Family Circle

Rebuilding trust within the family isn't easy, but it's possible. It starts with seeing each other clearly—not just for who we are today but for who we've been and who we can become. It means acknowledging the ways we've hurt each other and committing to healing those wounds.

Trusting the eyes behind you in the context of family means

believing that each member of the circle has a role to play and a responsibility to fulfill. It means protecting what's inside the circle and standing together against external threats. And it means trusting yourself enough to show up authentically, knowing that your presence strengthens the whole.

Rebuilding the family circle also requires patience. Trust isn't restored overnight; it's rebuilt moment by moment, through consistent actions and open communication. It means forgiving past mistakes while holding each other accountable for growth. Families who commit to this process find that their bonds become stronger than ever, capable of withstanding any challenge.

REFLECTION QUESTIONS

In what ways has your family built or broken trust over the years?

How can you contribute to strengthening the family circle in your own life?

What role do you play in protecting, nurturing, or guiding your family?

Action Steps

Identify one family member you've struggled to trust and take a step toward rebuilding that trust—whether it's through a conversation, an apology, or an act of kindness.

Spend time with an elder in your family. Ask them to share a story from their past and reflect on the lessons it holds.

Commit to showing vulnerability with at least one family member this week. Share something personal and invite them to do the same.

Notes

Chapter 4

Community Connectivity

"The construct of community catalyzes strong, deep feelings that can move people to action."
~Dr. Patricia Hill Collins

The Power of the Collective

Trust does not end at the boundaries of the family. Beyond those walls lies the broader community—a web of relationships, connections, and responsibilities that shape the way we live and grow together. If family is where we learn trust, community is where we practice it on a larger scale.

For people of African descent, the concept of community has always been deeply embedded in our way of life. We come from cultures where the collective good was prioritized, where each individual played a role in ensuring the survival and prosperity of the whole. Communities thrived on collaboration, with everyone contributing their skills, knowledge, and resources for the benefit of all. This approach to living created tightly woven networks of trust, where individuals understood that their success was tied to the success of the group.

But in modern times, this sense of communal trust has been eroded. The rise of individualism, coupled with systemic forces designed to fracture our unity, has left many of us feeling isolated and disconnected. The shift from "we" to "me" has created a vacuum, one where competition often takes precedence over collaboration, and mistrust undermines the potential for collective progress.

Despite these challenges, the power of the collective remains within reach. Rebuilding trust in our communities requires us to look back to our roots, drawing inspiration from the practices and philosophies that sustained our ancestors. It demands that we resist the narratives of individualism and reconnect with the principle that no one thrives alone. Communities built on trust, mutual respect, and shared values have the power to transform lives and create lasting legacies.

This chapter is about reconnecting with the power of the collective. It's about understanding that our greatest strength lies not in what we achieve individually, but in what we build together. Through stories, lessons, and lived experiences, we will explore how community connectivity can help us rediscover the trust that binds us.

The Fabled City of Pali

There is a powerful story about the City of Pali that perfectly illustrates the potential of community connectivity.

There was a traveler who had journeyed across the world, searching for a place he could call home. He had visited countless countries and cities, but everywhere he went, he saw homelessness, hopelessness, poverty, and devastation. Determined to find a better way of life, he kept traveling.

One day, while in the western portion of Africa, the traveler stumbled upon a city named Pali. From the moment he entered, he was astonished. Walking from one end of the city to the other, he spent the entire day marveling at what he saw. He had traveled far and wide, studying different cultures, cities, and nations, but he had never seen anything like this.

In Pali, every home was a mansion. The streets were immaculate, not a single piece of trash in sight. The people wore their finest kente cloth, exuding happiness and health. The children played safely in every corner of the city. There were no beggars, no signs of poverty, no disparity between rich and poor. Everyone seemed wealthy, content, and connected.

Finally, the traveler saw an elder sitting in the direction of the setting sun. Approaching him with reverence, the traveler asked, "Sir, forgive me for disturbing you, but I must ask—what is this place? Am I imagining what I see?"

The elder, intrigued, replied, "What troubles you, my son?"

The traveler explained, "Everywhere I've been in this world, there are always the rich, the middle class, and the poor. Poverty exists in every corner of the earth—except here. How is it possible that everyone in this city is wealthy and happy? How did you accomplish this?"

The elder smiled knowingly and began to share the secret of Pali. "Whenever someone comes to this great city and wishes to live here," he said, "we meet in council. The Council of Elders and the Mothers of the City come together to interview the individual, asking them questions about their character and intentions. Our spiritual priests and priestesses observe them, and we deliberate in closed session. If we determine that they possess the character and values we desire in our community, we welcome them as a resident.

"On the day they are accepted into the City of Pali, we hold a grand celebration. During this gathering, every resident brings two things: one brick and one dollar."

The traveler was intrigued. "How many people live in this city?" He asked.

The elder paused thoughtfully and replied, "Just over 100,000."

With a smile, he continued, "When you join us, those 100,000 bricks are used to build your mansion, and the $100,000 helps you start your life here in Pali. In return, you contribute your brick and dollar to help others who come after you."

This story, as retold by Ishakamusa Barashango and given to him by an Akan priest in West Africa, beautifully captures the essence of community and shared responsibility. It is a reminder of the lessons passed down through generations and the importance of preserving and honoring these teachings.

The Lessons of Pali

The City of Pali is more than just a fable—it's a vision of what communities can achieve when built on trust, contribution, and shared responsibility. At its core, Pali thrives because every resident understands the importance of interdependence. The brick and the dollar symbolize much more than material contributions; they represent a deeper commitment to the community's collective welfare. Each brick laid and every dollar given signify faith in the people who come next, a faith that creates an unbroken chain of trust and mutual support.

In modern communities, the lessons of Pali serve as a poignant reminder of the potential we often leave untapped. Imagine if every person in a neighborhood contributed their time, skills, or resources to uplift those around them. What could we accomplish if our focus shifted from individual success to collective progress? Pali challenges us to re-imagine what's possible, reminding us that true wealth lies in shared prosperity.

The metaphor of Pali also illuminates the damaging impact of individualism on modern society. When people prioritize personal gain over communal well-being, they erode the bonds that sustain trust. The "me-first" mentality undermines the very fabric of community, creating a cycle where those in need are left unsupported, and those who could help become isolated in their pursuit of self-interest. Pali asks us to reject this cycle and embrace a mindset where success is measured not by personal accumulation but by the strength and health of the collective.

Black Dot as a Catalyst for Community Empowerment

Black Dot quickly became more than a bookstore or coffee shop—it evolved into a cornerstone for community connection and empowerment. It served as a safe space where people could come together to discuss ideas, share stories, and find solutions to challenges facing the community. From its inception, Black Dot was grounded in a mission to foster trust and collective progress.

Promoting Literacy and Knowledge Sharing

At its heart, Black Dot was always about more than selling books. It was about promoting literacy and encouraging people to learn their history and engage with their culture. Bookshelves lined with works from African and African American authors provided access to stories and knowledge that were often excluded from mainstream spaces. Black Dot became a place where people could discover their heritage, explore new perspectives, and reconnect with the richness of their identities.

Through reading groups, author talks, and community workshops, Black Dot reinforced the idea that knowledge is power. By providing access to books and creating opportunities for discussion, it empowered individuals to think critically and apply those lessons to their personal and communal lives.

A Hub for Cultural Preservation

Black Dot also became a hub for preserving and celebrating African and African American culture. Art exhibits, musical performances, and cultural events transformed the space into a living tapestry of Black identity. These events weren't just entertainment—they were opportunities to pass down traditions, celebrate shared heritage, and strengthen the bonds of community.

One of the most powerful aspects of Black Dot's cultural role was its ability to bridge generational gaps. Elders shared their wisdom through storytelling and lectures, while younger generations brought fresh perspectives through creative expressions like poetry slams and spoken word nights. This intergenerational exchange not only preserved traditions but also infused them with new life.

Expanding the Vision: The Black Dot Leadership Academy

Building upon the foundation of the Black Dot Cultural Center, the creation of the Black Dot Cultural Center and Leadership Academy, a 501(c)(3) nonprofit organization, marked a significant expansion of its mission. This next chapter was driven by the vision of extending the center's impact beyond its physical walls and equipping the community with tools for long-term empowerment.

The Leadership Academy focuses on nurturing future leaders through programs that emphasize civic engagement, cultural awareness, and personal growth. By offering workshops, mentorship opportunities, and leadership training, the Academy serves as a space where individuals can develop the skills and knowledge necessary to drive positive change within their communities.

This evolution underscores the power of collective trust and shared purpose. Just as Black Dot was built on the trust and contributions of its supporters, the Leadership Academy carries forward that legacy, fostering a new generation of leaders rooted in the values of cultural pride, community service, and collaboration.

Economic Empowerment Through Community Support

Black Dot wasn't just a cultural center—it was also a small business that prioritized economic empowerment. By sourcing products from Black-owned businesses and promoting local entrepreneurs, Black Dot became a platform for economic development within the community. It hosted vendor markets, business expos, and financial literacy workshops, helping residents turn their ideas into sustainable ventures.

The center's commitment to economic empowerment extended beyond its walls. It inspired patrons to support other Black-owned businesses, creating a ripple effect that strengthened the local economy. Black Dot's success showed what was possible when communities rallied around their own, proving that economic self-determination could coexist with cultural enrichment.

Fostering Dialogue and Social Change

Perhaps one of the most transformative aspects of Black Dot was its role as a space for dialogue and social change. It became a gathering place where people could have honest conversations about issues affecting their lives—racism, education, policing, economic inequality, and more. These conversations weren't just academic; they were action-oriented, often leading to grassroots initiatives and collaborative efforts to address local challenges.

For example, Black Dot organized town hall meetings that brought together community members, activists, and local leaders to discuss pressing issues. These events weren't about assigning blame—they were about finding solutions. The trust cultivated within the space allowed people to express their ideas openly, creating a foundation for collective action.

A Symbol of What's Possible

Looking back, I realize that Black Dot was more than just a center—it was a symbol of what's possible when trust is present in a community. It demonstrated that with vision, collaboration, and shared values, communities could create spaces that uplift and empower everyone involved. Black Dot wasn't just my dream; it became a shared vision that reflected the hopes and aspirations of the people who supported it.

The addition of the Leadership Academy represents the next step in that shared vision. By focusing on leadership, education, and community engagement, it builds upon the foundation laid by the Cultural Center, ensuring that the work of empowerment continues for generations to come. Together, they stand as a testament to the transformative power of community connectivity and the enduring importance of trusting the eyes behind you.

Rebuilding Community Trust

The story of Black Dot, like the City of Pali, demonstrates what's possible when trust is present in a community. Trusting the eyes behind you in a community context means believing that others have your back, even when you can't see what lies ahead. It's a leap of faith, a mutual agreement that everyone will contribute their part for the greater good.

Rebuilding trust in a community is no small task. It requires intentionality, transparency, and the willingness to address past wounds. Many communities have experienced breaches of trust—

whether through systemic injustices, broken promises, or internal conflicts. These fractures can leave individuals feeling disillusioned and disconnected, making the process of restoration all the more challenging.

One of the first steps to rebuilding trust is creating spaces where people feel safe to connect and communicate. This is why spaces like Black Dot are so vital. They provide a neutral ground where individuals can come together, share their experiences, and work toward common goals. These spaces aren't just physical—they're symbolic. They represent the possibility of connection, the belief that trust can be rebuilt one relationship at a time.

Rebuilding trust also requires action. Words alone won't mend broken bonds; they must be followed by consistent, visible efforts to support and uplift the community. This could mean organizing grassroots initiatives, addressing systemic barriers, or simply showing up for one another in times of need. Trust is built through action, through the tangible demonstration of care and commitment. In my own journey, people like Jhavaun, Marie, and Robin were the eyes behind me. They saw what I couldn't see and helped me take leaps I wouldn't have taken on my own. But just as I've received support, I've also tried to be the eyes behind others, encouraging them to trust in their own potential and contribute to the collective good. Trust flows both ways, creating a cycle of giving and receiving that strengthens the fabric of the community.

The lessons of Pali remind us that community is about more than proximity—it's about connection. It's about showing up for each other with our bricks and dollars, with our hands and hearts, with our trust and our action. When we rebuild trust, we rebuild the foundation of our collective power, creating communities where everyone can thrive.

REFLECTION QUESTIONS

How does the concept of the City of Pali inspire you to think differently about your role in your community?

In what ways can you contribute your "brick and dollar" to the betterment of your community?

Think about a time when you supported someone or were supported by others. How did trust play a role in that experience?

What lessons from the story of Black Dot Cultural Center resonate most with your vision of community connectivity?

Action Steps

Identify a Need in Your Community: Look around your neighborhood or local community. Is there an area where trust has been broken or where collaboration is lacking? Brainstorm ways you can contribute to rebuilding that trust or addressing that need.

Support a Community Initiative: Find an organization, event, or group in your community that aligns with the principles of trust and shared responsibility. Get involved by volunteering your time, donating resources, or spreading awareness.

Host a Conversation: Organize a small gathering to discuss the themes of community trust and connectivity. Use the lessons of Pali and Black Dot as starting points for reflection and brainstorming.
Mentor or Be Mentored: Identify someone you can mentor or learn from within your community. Building relationships across generations fosters trust and strengthens communal bonds.

Notes

Chapter 5

The Spiritual Dimensions of Trust

"Faith is taking the first step even when you don't see the whole staircase."

— Dr. Martin Luther King Jr.

Trust as a Bridge to Our Higher Selves

Trust is one of the most powerful forces in our lives. It is the foundation of every meaningful connection we form—with others, with ourselves, and with the unseen forces that guide our path. It serves as a bridge, carrying us over fear and uncertainty and leading us toward clarity, love, and purpose.

While trust often begins externally, its deepest and most transformative dimensions are spiritual. For some, this trust takes the form of prayer—a conversation with God or the divine that opens us to guidance, strength, and gratitude. For others, it is rooted in manifestation—the intentional act of envisioning a desired future and aligning oneself to achieve it. Although prayer and manifestation may appear distinct, they share a common purpose: cultivating trust in the unseen while driving us toward action.

Spiritual trust challenges us to believe in more than what we can see or control. It invites us to lean on the wisdom of our ancestors, the presence of the divine, and the strength within ourselves. Trust is not passive; it grows through experience, reflection, and deliberate effort. It is a commitment to keep moving forward, even when the path ahead is uncertain.

In this chapter, we will explore how spiritual trust—expressed through prayer, manifestation, and action—connects us to our higher selves, strengthens our bond with our ancestors, and creates legacies for future generations.

The Journey to the Higher Self

To understand spiritual trust, we must first turn inward. The journey to the higher self begins by confronting our fears, insecurities, and doubts and trusting that we are capable of rising above them. It calls us to believe in the possibility of transformation and to recognize that we carry the seeds of clarity, compassion, and strength within us.

In African spirituality, the higher self is deeply intertwined with the wisdom of our ancestors. The ancestors are not merely figures of the past; they are ever-present guides, offering protection, insight, and resilience. Their struggles and triumphs remind us that we are connected to a lineage of strength. Trusting the higher self, then, is also trusting the eyes behind you—the understanding that the courage and wisdom of those who came before us continue to support us today.

In Christianity, the higher self is often framed through faith in God. This trust encourages believers to see themselves as vessels of divine purpose, capable of transcending fear and doubt. Trust in God is not passive; it requires active engagement with life, aligning one's actions with principles of love, service, and faith.

Prayer and manifestation are two pathways to connect with the higher self. Prayer creates space for divine connection, offering moments of stillness and clarity. Manifestation allows us to imagine the future we want and take steps toward it. These practices are not opposites; they are complementary. Both call us to trust in the unseen while taking action to bring our visions to life.

Consider a young man at a crossroads in life. Unsure of which direction to take, he turns inward for guidance. Through prayer, he asks for clarity and strength, trusting that divine wisdom will reveal itself. At the same time, he visualizes his future—one filled with purpose and fulfillment. Each step he takes, however small, moves him closer to that vision. His trust in the process, supported by prayer and his own actions, transforms hesitation into momentum.

Spiritual trust connects us to our higher selves, reminding us that transformation is possible when we align our beliefs, intentions, and actions.

Honoring the Eyes Behind You

To trust spiritually is to honor the eyes behind you—the ancestors who paved the way for your existence. In African traditions, this is more than an acknowledgment of the past; it is an active relationship with those who came before us. Ancestors are not distant or disconnected; they are alive in spirit, offering wisdom, strength, and guidance.

Honoring the ancestors often involves rituals such as pouring libation or sharing their stories. These acts are not about worship but about gratitude and connection. They remind us that the resilience we draw upon today is the result of their sacrifices. To honor them is to trust that their strength lives on within us, guiding us forward.

When I poured libation before opening Black Dot Cultural Center, I wasn't just performing a ritual—I was anchoring myself in the legacy of my ancestors. I trusted that their wisdom would guide me through the uncertainty of creating something new. At the same time, I visualized the center as a space where their stories and sacrifices could live on. In that moment, prayer and manifestation were not separate—they were interwoven, forming a bridge between the past and the future.

Honoring our ancestors is an act of trust that reinforces our connection to the legacy of strength and resilience that sustains us. It reminds us that we are never alone, no matter how heavy the journey may feel.

The Power of Prayer and Manifestation

Prayer and manifestation are two practices that reflect the deepest dimensions of spiritual trust. Prayer is the act of opening oneself to divine guidance, asking for clarity, strength, or direction. Manifestation begins with envisioning a future that aligns with one's purpose and taking steps to bring that vision to life. Together, they form a powerful framework for trust and action.

The poem Footprints in the Sand beautifully illustrates this concept.

Footprints in the Sand

One night I dreamed I was walking along the beach with the Lord.
Many scenes from my life flashed across the sky.
In each scene, I noticed footprints in the sand.
Sometimes there were two sets of footprints,
Other times there were one set of footprints.
This bothered me because I noticed
that during the low periods of my life,
when I was suffering from anguish, sorrow, or defeat,
I could see only one set of footprints.
So I said to the Lord,
"You promised me, Lord,
that if I followed you,
you would walk with me always.
But I have noticed that during the most trying periods of my life
there have only been one set of footprints in the sand.
Why, when I needed you most, you have not been there for me?"
The Lord replied,
"The times when you have seen only one set of footprints
is when I carried you."

The poem's message reminds us that trust does not mean we will never face challenges. Instead, it assures us that we are supported, even when we cannot see it. Prayer and manifestation require this same kind of trust—a belief that we are not alone and that the divine will meet us in our efforts.

When I prayed for Black Dot Cultural Center, I trusted that God and my ancestors would guide me. But I also knew I had to move my feet. I imagined the space, wrote down my plans, and took deliberate steps to make it real. Manifestation is not just about envisioning the future; it is about aligning your actions with your vision and doing the work to bring it to life.

Prayer and manifestation teach us that trust is not passive—it is an active, dynamic process that requires faith and effort in equal measure.

Faith, Legacy, and the Future

Spiritual trust is not bound by the limits of the present moment. It is a bridge that connects the wisdom of the past, the actions of today, and the aspirations of tomorrow. This trust extends beyond personal growth; it becomes the foundation upon which we build legacies that endure. Legacy is the embodiment of spiritual trust in action—a conscious decision to pass down traditions, values, and stories that inspire and empower future generations.

When we honor our ancestors, pray with intention, and manifest with purpose, we are not simply shaping our own lives; we are planting seeds for those who will come after us. Legacy is a gift, carefully cultivated, and spiritual trust is what allows us to believe that our efforts will bear fruit, even if we never see the full harvest. Consider a family that gathers each year to reflect on their shared history. Around the dinner table, elders recount stories of survival—tales of great-grandparents who weathered storms of injustice, built communities from nothing, and created opportunities for their children. These stories are not just memories; they are lessons. They remind younger generations that resilience is in their blood, that they, too, can overcome life's challenges because they are part of something greater. Legacy, in this sense, is not only about material wealth or accomplishments; it is about passing down the trust that the family has what it takes to thrive, no matter the circumstances.

Spiritual trust invites us to live with an awareness that our actions today ripple outward, influencing lives far beyond our own. When we pray or manifest, we often think of the immediate outcomes we hope to achieve. But these practices are also about aligning ourselves with a broader vision, one that includes the future we are creating for others. Every choice we make, every value we uphold, every tradition we pass down becomes a thread in the fabric of legacy. For example, imagine a young woman starting her own business, driven by a desire to uplift her community. Her work is more than entrepreneurial—it is spiritual. Through prayer, she seeks wisdom and courage. Through manifestation, she visualizes her success and the impact it will have on her community. Her actions—mentoring young people, reinvesting in local initiatives, and honoring the lessons of her ancestors—become a living legacy. She is not just building a business; she is creating a foundation for others to stand on. Legacy is also about the courage to break cycles and start anew. For many, spiritual trust involves healing from past wounds—both personal and generational. It requires the faith to believe that the future can be different, that the patterns of pain or limitation that may have defined previous generations do not have to define what comes next. This, too, is an act of spiritual trust: believing in the unseen possibility of a better tomorrow and taking deliberate steps to make it real. Spiritual trust as legacy calls us to be intentional about the values we live by. When we choose to honor our ancestors, we teach the next generation about the importance of remembering where they come from. When we pray with intention, we model the power of faith and perseverance. When we manifest with purpose, we show that dreams require both vision and effort. And when we act with integrity, we demonstrate that trust—both in ourselves and in the divine—is the foundation of any lasting impact.

Legacy is not limited to grand gestures or monumental achievements. It is found in the everyday acts of trust and love that shape our families, our communities, and our world. It is the decision to listen to a child, to share a story of struggle and triumph, to take one small action that makes life better for someone else. It is the quiet, consistent practice of living a life that honors the past, empowers the present, and inspires the future.

Spiritual trust reminds us that we are part of a continuum—a thread in a tapestry that began long before us and will continue long after we are gone. By embracing this perspective, we are freed from the pressure to achieve everything in our lifetime. Instead, we are invited to focus on the contributions we can make today, trusting that they will weave into a legacy that will support and uplift generations to come.

Imagine standing in a garden you may never fully see bloom. You plant seeds, water them, and nurture the soil, trusting that the work you do today will one day grow into something beautiful. That is legacy: an act of faith that transcends the self, rooted in the belief that the future can—and will—flourish.

Spiritual trust in legacy is an invitation. It calls us to see ourselves not just as individuals but as part of a greater whole. It challenges us to live with intention, knowing that our actions ripple outward in ways we may never fully understand. And it reminds us that the stories we tell, the values we embody, and the steps we take today are shaping a future that honors the past, empowers the present, and inspires those who follow.

Conclusion: A Commitment to Trust

Spiritual trust is a journey, one that invites us to engage deeply with ourselves, the divine, and the unseen forces that shape our path. It is not a single act or moment but an ongoing commitment to believe in what we cannot yet see and to act with faith, even in uncertainty.

At its core, spiritual trust is about partnership. It calls on us to align prayer and manifestation, faith and action. Prayer opens us to divine connection, offering moments of clarity and strength. Manifestation helps us envision the life we want to create. But both practices remind us of a greater truth: trust requires us to take steps forward, even when the road ahead is unclear.

Legacy is perhaps the most profound expression of spiritual trust. The prayers we say, the visions we manifest, and the actions we take today create a foundation for those who come after us. By honoring the past and engaging fully with the present, we shape a future rooted in resilience, love, and purpose.

There will be moments when doubt creeps in or when the weight of life feels too great. In those times, spiritual trust reminds us that we are not alone. The divine, our ancestors, and the strength within us are all carrying us forward. As Footprints in the Sand illustrates, there are moments when we may not see the second set of footprints, but that does not mean we are walking alone—it means we are being carried.

As you close this chapter, I invite you to reflect on the role of trust in your own life. How have prayer or manifestation guided your steps? What unseen forces have shaped your journey? What legacy are you building today that will empower future generations? Spiritual trust is not the absence of challenges; it is the courage to face them. It is the understanding that our faith, our actions, and the unseen forces that guide us all work together to create lives of meaning and impact. Trust is the bridge between where we are and where we are meant to be.

REFLECTION QUESTIONS

How has prayer or manifestation shaped your journey?

What practices or rituals help you connect to your ancestors or the divine?

In what areas of your life do you need to cultivate greater trust?

What legacy are you building for future generations?

How can you align your actions more closely with your intentions and beliefs?

Action Steps

Create a Prayer or Manifestation Ritual: Dedicate time each day to pray or visualize your goals. Use this practice to reflect on your intentions and align your actions with your aspirations.

Honor the Ancestors: Create a meaningful way to acknowledge your ancestors—pour libation, light a candle, or spend time reflecting on their stories.

Take Action Toward a Vision: Identify one goal you've been holding back on and take a deliberate step toward it this week. Trust that the process will unfold as you move forward.

Write Your Vision: Spend time journaling about your dreams. Be specific and include practical steps you can take to make them a reality.
Reflect on Trust: At the end of each day, reflect on how trust influenced your actions and decisions. Write down one instance where you leaned into trust.

Notes

Chapter 6

The Need for Community Trust & Healing

"The recovery of African memory is the beginning of the restoration of African humanity." — *Dr. John Henrik Clarke*

Trust Across Time

Trusting the eyes behind you requires understanding not just where you are but where you've been—and for African-descended people, our history is far richer and more complex than the narratives of enslavement and segregation often suggest. Our story begins in Africa, where we built civilizations rooted in culture, spirituality, and communal connection for thousands of years. These societies traded in gold and ivory, developed governance systems, and contributed to human knowledge in mathematics, science, art, and philosophy. This uninterrupted history of thriving communities was disrupted by the transatlantic slave trade, a violent rupture that sought to sever not only our physical connections but also our ties to culture, spirituality, and identity. Yet, even through the enslavement period, Jim Crow, and segregation, the thread of trust and resilience persisted.

As we reflect on the journey from our origins in Africa to the struggles and triumphs of life in America, it becomes clear that trust—within ourselves, within our families, and within our communities—has been a constant force. This chapter explores how historical disruptions reshaped our collective trust and identity and why reclaiming those ancestral principles is essential for healing and progress today.

Africa: The Original Circle of Trust

Before the disruption of enslavement, African civilizations thrived on communal values and interdependence. The City of Pali, though a fable, reflects the essence of this reality. Empires such as Ghana, Mali, and Songhai were built on principles of shared responsibility, trade, and cultural exchange. The Akan people, the largest ethnic group in present-day Ghana, exemplify this legacy with their emphasis on unity, spirituality, and collective care.

The Adinkra symbol Sankofa, meaning "Go back and fetch it," reminds us that the wisdom of our ancestors is not lost—it is waiting to be reclaimed. The story of the City of Pali, as retold by Ishakamusa Barashango and originating from an Akan priest, teaches us that thriving communities are possible when every member contributes to the collective good. These lessons from Africa remind us that trust and interconnectedness are not new ideas—they are deeply rooted in our heritage.

Marimba Ani, in her work Yurugu, emphasizes the importance of cultural cohesion, noting that pre-colonial African societies were sustained by their shared values and spiritual connection. "To lose this connection is to lose our center," she warns, underscoring the need to reclaim these principles as a foundation for rebuilding trust today.

The Disruption: Enslavement and the Fracturing of Trust

The transatlantic slave trade was not merely a historical event; it was an existential assault on the identity, autonomy, and cohesion of African communities. Over 12 million Africans were forcibly removed from their homelands, crammed into the bowels of ships under inhumane conditions, and sold into a system designed to commodify and dehumanize them. The physical brutality of enslavement—the whippings, forced labor, and deprivation—was only one part of the trauma. Equally devastating was the psychological and spiritual rupture inflicted on those torn from their families, cultures, and communities.

Marimba Ani describes this systematic dismantling of cultural integrity in her seminal work, Yurugu, noting that enslaved Africans were stripped of their identities and forcibly assimilated into roles that erased their humanity. This process, which she terms "cultural asphyxiation," sought to sever the enslaved from their spiritual foundations and communal values. European colonizers deliberately targeted the bonds of trust that underpinned African societies, isolating individuals and fostering mistrust to weaken resistance. This destruction of collective identity was a strategic weapon in maintaining control.

Yet, even in the face of this brutality, trust endured. Enslaved Africans preserved their humanity through cultural resilience. Storytelling became a vessel for preserving history and transmitting moral lessons across generations. Spirituals and work songs, often encoded with messages of resistance, served as a source of hope and solidarity. These practices were more than mere survival mechanisms—they were acts of defiance, a refusal to let the oppressors sever the ties that bound them to one another and to their ancestors.

The creation of new circles of trust within the constraints of plantation life exemplifies this resilience. Families, though often fractured by forced separations, were reimagined through the adoption of fictive kinship systems. "Mama" and "Papa" roles were assumed by those who could provide guidance and care to younger or orphaned individuals, creating new family structures built on trust and mutual support. Enslaved communities also forged bonds through communal rituals, such as clandestine religious gatherings, where they found solace and strength in their shared faith.

The endurance of these bonds highlights the power of trust as a lifeline in the darkest of circumstances. Dr. Vincent Harding reminds us, "We were never meant to survive, but we did—and we thrived because of the power of community." His words capture the essence of how trust functioned as an anchor amid chaos. It enabled enslaved Africans to maintain a sense of humanity and dignity in a system that sought to strip them of both.

    Furthermore, resistance was often grounded in communal trust. From revolts like those led by Nat Turner and Gabriel Prosser to the establishment of maroon communities by escaped enslaved people, acts of defiance relied on coordinated efforts and unyielding faith in one another. These rebellions were dangerous, and betrayal could mean death, but the shared goal of freedom reinforced the bonds of trust necessary to resist oppression.

    Spirituality also played a critical role in sustaining trust. While enslavers sought to use religion as a tool of subjugation, many enslaved Africans reinterpreted Christian teachings to align with their own values of liberation and justice. This syncretism blended African spiritual traditions with Christian motifs, creating a theology of resistance that affirmed their humanity and right to freedom. The belief that a higher power was on their side strengthened communal bonds, as faith became both a refuge and a rallying cry.

    The trauma of enslavement, however, left scars that extend across generations. The deliberate fracturing of families, suppression of languages, and erasure of cultural practices created intergenerational wounds that continue to shape the African diaspora's relationship with trust today. Yet, as Dr. Joy DeGruy explores in Post Traumatic Slave Syndrome, acknowledging and addressing these wounds is essential to reclaiming our collective identity and rebuilding the bonds disrupted by systemic oppression.

    The resilience of enslaved Africans is a testament to the enduring power of trust. Despite every effort to destroy their connections to each other and their heritage, they preserved the principles of community, care, and faith, passing them down to future generations.

Their legacy is one of unyielding strength, a reminder that even in the most dehumanizing conditions, trust can serve as a foundation for survival, resistance, and ultimately, liberation.

Jim Crow and Segregation: Rebuilding the Circle

In the aftermath of slavery, African Americans faced the systemic racism of Jim Crow laws and segregation. These eras, though oppressive, required Black communities to rely on one another more than ever. Excluded from white-owned businesses, schools, and institutions, African Americans created their own systems of survival and empowerment, turning necessity into a catalyst for innovation and resilience.

Building Institutions of Trust and Progress

Black Wall Streets, Historically Black Colleges and Universities (HBCUs), and the Black Church became the pillars of Black communities. These institutions were more than just places of commerce, education, or worship—they were the epicenters of cultural, social, and economic life. In towns like Greenwood, Oklahoma—home to the original Black Wall Street—African Americans built thriving economies. Doctors, lawyers, teachers, and business owners operated within these communities, where Black dollars circulated multiple times before leaving.

This economic self-reliance was critical in fostering communal trust. Dr. Claud Anderson underscores the importance of this economic model, stating, "Wealth is the foundation of empowerment. When communities keep their dollars circulating among themselves, they create opportunities for growth and self-determination." Segregation, while born of systemic injustice, inadvertently forced African Americans to develop robust ecosystems that reflected the values and priorities of their communities.

HBCUs, established during Reconstruction, became incubators for the leaders of the Civil Rights Movement. Figures like Dr. Martin Luther King Jr., Thurgood Marshall, and Diane Nash emerged from these institutions, which instilled not only academic excellence but also a sense of social responsibility and collective purpose. The Black Church, too, was a cornerstone of community life. It served as a space of spiritual refuge, political organization, and cultural expression, reinforcing the bonds of trust within Black communities.

Circulating Wealth and Rebuilding Trust

During segregation, Black dollars circulated extensively

within Black communities, creating opportunities and fostering a sense of shared responsibility. This economic model exemplified the principles of collective care and mutual uplift. Businesses thrived not just because of their products but because of the trust they cultivated among their customers and the community at large.

The resilience of Black communities during this period is a testament to the enduring power of trust. Despite systemic efforts to oppress and marginalize, African Americans built institutions and systems that preserved their dignity, strengthened their resilience, and passed these principles on to future generations.

Overcoming Threats to Progress

However, these thriving communities were not without threats. The Tulsa Race Massacre of 1921, among other acts of white supremacist violence, targeted Black prosperity with the intent to destroy it. Such events were devastating, yet they revealed the deep trust and strength within Black communities. Families rebuilt, institutions regrouped, and the principles of collective care persisted.

Dr. W.E.B. Du Bois captured this dynamic when he wrote in The Souls of Black Folk: "The function of the Negro college is not simply to teach bread-winning, but to teach life." This sentiment encapsulates the broader mission of Black institutions during segregation: not just to survive, but to equip the community with tools for lasting empowerment.

The Legacy of Jim Crow and Segregation

This period, though marked by immense struggle, demonstrated the strength and resilience of communal trust. It was a time when African Americans turned systemic exclusion into an opportunity to innovate, preserve cultural identity, and foster collective progress. These lessons remain relevant today, reminding us of the power of trust to create thriving ecosystems of care and support. As we reflect on the era of Jim Crow and segregation, it becomes clear that these moments in history are not just about oppression—they are also about the enduring power of trust, self-reliance, and the will to create something lasting in the face of adversity. These values form the bedrock of the progress we strive for today and illuminate the path forward for future generations.

Integration: A New Opportunity, A New Challenge

The Civil Rights Movement ushered in profound changes, breaking down barriers that had long kept African Americans from accessing equal opportunities. Landmark legislation like the Civil Rights Act of 1964, the Voting Rights Act of 1965, and affirmative action initiatives opened doors to education, careers, and housing in spaces that had been previously denied. These victories, fought for with blood, sweat, and tears, symbolized the progress of a people determined to secure their rightful place in society.

However, integration was not without its challenges. The close-knit ecosystems of Black businesses, schools, and institutions, which had flourished during segregation, began to erode. Freed from the necessity of relying on Black-owned establishments, many Black Americans sought opportunities in integrated spaces. While this was a natural progression, it inadvertently weakened the communal infrastructure that had long supported Black progress.

The Rise of Individualism

Integration brought with it a shift toward individualism. During segregation, the ethos of "each one, teach one" ensured that success was shared, and progress was collective. But as opportunities expanded, the focus shifted to personal advancement. The drive to succeed often came at the expense of communal bonds, leaving gaps in the trust and support networks that had defined Black communities for generations.

Dr. Martin Luther King Jr. foresaw this risk, cautioning that integration needed to be accompanied by economic justice. "We are integrating into a burning house," he warned, highlighting the dangers of pursuing integration without addressing the systemic inequities that had long marginalized Black communities. King urged the movement to not only fight for access but also preserve the cultural and communal strength that had been its backbone.

The Economic Toll of Integration

The economic impact of integration on Black communities was profound. Black-owned businesses, which had thrived during segregation, struggled to compete with larger, white-owned corporations that now had access to Black consumers. This shift led to the closure of many Black establishments, weakening the economic foundation of Black neighborhoods.

Dr. Claud Anderson argues that integration diluted Black economic power by redirecting resources away from Black businesses and into mainstream markets. "Economic self-sufficiency is the key to empowerment," he writes, emphasizing that true progress requires maintaining control over the economic engines of the community. Integration, while providing access to new opportunities, often came at the cost of this control.

Cultural Disconnection and the Loss of Institutions

Integration also had a cultural impact, as many Black Americans moved into predominantly white spaces to access better schools, housing, and jobs. While these moves were understandable, they often resulted in a disconnection from the cultural institutions that had provided a sense of identity and belonging. The Black Church, Black schools, and community centers that had once been hubs of collective trust and progress saw their influence wane as individuals sought opportunities outside of their communities.

This disconnection contributed to a gradual weakening of the communal mindset that had been so integral to Black survival and success during segregation. The focus on individual advancement, while beneficial in many ways, left communities vulnerable to systemic inequities that persisted despite legal progress.

The Cost of Unhealed Wounds

One of the most significant challenges we face today is the lack of collective healing. The trauma of slavery, segregation, and systemic racism has left deep scars that remain unaddressed. These wounds are not just historical—they continue to shape the lives of Black Americans, influencing relationships, opportunities, and community dynamics.

Understanding Collective Trauma

Marimba Ani underscores the importance of addressing collective trauma, writing, "Healing begins with understanding our collective pain and re-centering ourselves in the values that sustained us." This trauma is not merely individual but deeply communal, passed down through generations in the form of mistrust, internalized oppression, and fractured relationships.

The cultural shift toward individualism has compounded this challenge. When we prioritize personal success over collective well-being, we lose the sense of shared responsibility that is essential for healing. The bonds that once held us together weaken, leaving many of us feeling isolated and unsupported in the face of systemic inequities.

Healing as a Foundation for Trust

Healing is foundational to trust. Without addressing the

wounds of the past, it is difficult to build the trust needed to move forward as a community. This healing must go beyond emotional and psychological recovery—it must also be structural. It involves rebuilding the institutions, systems, and relationships that were fractured by integration and systemic racism.

Dr. Joy DeGruy's concept of Post-Traumatic Slave Syndrome highlights the intergenerational impact of trauma and the need for intentional healing practices. "The trauma of slavery and systemic racism has left a legacy that we must actively work to heal," she writes. This work requires acknowledging the pain, creating safe spaces for dialogue, and fostering a culture of collective care and accountability.

Reclaiming Sankofa: Wisdom from the Past

The Adinkra symbol Sankofa, meaning "Go back and fetch it," offers a powerful framework for reclaiming the values and practices that sustained our ancestors. This principle reminds us that the wisdom of the past is not lost—it is waiting to be retrieved and adapted to today's challenges.

Returning to Communal Principles

Rebuilding trust within the Black community begins with revisiting the communal principles that defined our identity during segregation and in Africa. Supporting Black-owned businesses, investing in Black institutions, and fostering a culture of collective care are essential steps in this process. These actions not only strengthen economic foundations but also rebuild the trust and connections that are critical for progress.

Marimba Ani emphasizes the importance of reconnecting with our cultural essence, writing, "We must return to the spiritual and communal principles that anchored our ancestors." This return is not about nostalgia but about creating a future rooted in resilience, authenticity, and collective empowerment.

Addressing Systemic Barriers

Reclaiming Sankofa also means addressing the systemic barriers that continue to hinder progress. This involves advocating for policy changes that reflect our values and priorities, as well as creating our own systems and solutions. The lessons of the past show us that self-reliance and communal trust are powerful tools for overcoming external challenges.

A Blueprint for the Future

The story of the City of Pali serves as a blueprint for what is possible when communities prioritize trust and shared responsibility. By building systems that reflect the principles of Sankofa, we can create spaces of empowerment, healing, and progress that honor our past while addressing the needs of the present.

Conclusion: Trust as the Foundation of Healing and Progress

Our history, from Africa to the present day, is a testament to the enduring power of trust, resilience, and collective care. Even in the face of systemic barriers, our communities have found ways to thrive, leaning on the strength of shared values and the wisdom of our ancestors. The lessons of the past remind us that we are capable of not only surviving but flourishing when we trust in one another and invest in our collective future.

Today, we see signs of this resilience everywhere. Grassroots organizations are mobilizing to address systemic inequities. Black-owned businesses are reclaiming their place as cornerstones of economic empowerment. Cultural movements are reigniting pride in our heritage, and young leaders are carrying forward the legacy of activism, innovation, and community building.

Healing the wounds of the past is not just a process of restoration—it is a pathway to transformation. By reclaiming the principles of Sankofa, we honor the values that sustained our ancestors while charting a new course for generations to come. We have the tools, the knowledge, and the spirit to rebuild trust within our communities, creating spaces where every individual feels valued, supported, and empowered.

Imagine a future where Black communities thrive as centers of culture, commerce, and creativity. A future where trust flows freely, bridging generations and strengthening bonds across neighborhoods, cities, and nations. This vision is within our grasp, but it requires action—a commitment to trusting the eyes behind us, seeing the potential within us, and believing in the legacy we can create together. Let us move forward with the confidence that we are not alone. We are guided by the resilience of our ancestors, the strength of our shared history, and the potential of our collective future. Trust is not just a bridge between where we are and where we want to be—it is the foundation of the thriving, empowered communities we are destined to build.

REFLECTION QUESTIONS

How has trust, or the lack thereof, shaped your sense of community?

What lessons from African traditions resonate with how we can rebuild trust today?

In what ways can we balance reclaiming cultural principles with addressing modern challenges?

How has the narrative of integration influenced your understanding of community trust?

What steps can you take to participate in healing and restoring trust in your community?

Action Steps

Engage in Local Community Initiatives: Join or support grassroots organizations that work to rebuild trust and equity in Black communities.

Study African Traditions: Explore the values and systems of African civilizations to understand the foundational principles of community trust.

Support Black-Owned Businesses: Actively invest in Black-owned establishments to strengthen economic trust and resilience.

Host Intergenerational Dialogues: Create spaces where elders and youth can share stories, lessons, and perspectives on community trust.

Advocate for Policy Change: Support policies that promote equity, transparency, and community well-being at local and national levels.

Notes

Chapter 7

Trust & Legacy Bridging Generations

"The seeds we plant today will become the trees that shelter future generations."

– Dr. Maya Angelou

The Seeds We Plant

Legacy is more than material wealth—it is the values, wisdom, and connections we cultivate and pass to the next generation. For African-descended people, legacy holds a special significance, serving as both a gift from our ancestors and a responsibility to our descendants. It is a living thread that ties together our past, present, and future.

At the heart of legacy is trust. It is the foundation that strengthens relationships, sustains communities, and ensures that the bridge connecting generations endures. Without trust, the transmission of legacy becomes fragmented, its power diluted by fear, doubt, or neglect. When we reflect on trust and legacy, we must consider how each generation contributes to the next, either reinforcing or weakening the bonds that link them.

The principles of legacy are as old as the empires and villages of Africa. In the Ghana Empire, for example, trust in shared responsibility and communal care sustained trade and prosperity. These lessons from history remind us that the seeds we plant today shape not only our lives but also the futures of those who come after us. Dr. John Henrik Clarke once said, "A people's relationship to their history is the same as a child's relationship to its mother. Without a historical context, you have no direction." Legacy provides that direction—a compass rooted in trust, guiding us toward a future that honors our past.

This chapter examines how trust shapes legacy as both an inheritance and an active creation. By exploring the lessons of our ancestors, the responsibilities of today, and the possibilities of tomorrow, we ask: What seeds are we planting to ensure our legacy thrives?

The Legacy of Trust:
Inheriting Ancestral Trust

Trust is one of the most profound gifts passed down through generations. For African-descended people, this inheritance is steeped in the wisdom and resilience of our ancestors, who preserved trust even in the face of unimaginable adversity.

During the enslavement period, rituals, oral traditions, and spiritual practices became essential vessels of trust. These traditions helped enslaved Africans maintain their humanity and sustain their communities. Even amid the dehumanizing conditions of slavery, they planted seeds of trust that continue to bear fruit today. The griots of African culture embodied this inheritance. As storytellers and historians, they safeguarded communal knowledge, passing it down through generations. Through their stories, they nurtured a sense of identity, connection, and trust in the enduring power of the community.

Dr. Molefi Kete Asante reminds us, "History is a continuum, and our connection to it gives us the power to transform the present." Ancestral trust, therefore, is not simply about remembering the past—it is about using the wisdom of history to empower the present and shape the future.

The Burden of Shame and Silence

For many African-descended people, the weight of history is not only one of trauma, but also of shame—an insidious emotion that distorts identity and disconnects individuals from their cultural heritage. This shame stems from centuries of dehumanization, systemic oppression, and societal conditioning designed to portray Blackness as inferior or undesirable. The atrocities of slavery, the injustices of Jim Crow, and the enduring persistence of systemic racism have left intergenerational scars that are often difficult to confront or even acknowledge. Shame was weaponized as a deliberate tool of oppression. Enslaved Africans were stripped of their names, languages, and cultural practices—acts designed to sever their ties to heritage and instill feelings of inferiority. W.E.B. Du Bois captured this conflict in his concept of "double consciousness," describing the painful dual awareness of being both a person and a caricature shaped by societal stereotypes. This tension created an enduring struggle to reclaim authenticity while navigating the constraints of a white-dominated society.

In response to this shame, many elders, driven by love and a desire to shield their children from pain, chose silence. They refrained from sharing the horrors they endured, such as the violence of Jim Crow, the terror of lynch mobs, or the daily indignities of systemic discrimination. While this silence protected younger generations from direct exposure to trauma, it inadvertently created a void, leaving many disconnected from the resilience, strength, and strategies that had enabled survival. This silence was a double-edged sword. On one hand, it allowed families to focus on future opportunities, encouraging education and professional advancement. On the other, it left subsequent generations unaware of the communal struggles that laid the groundwork for their progress. Without these stories, the triumphs of survival and the lessons embedded within them are forever lost.

The consequences of this silence are profound. Shame and disconnection from Blackness often manifest as discomfort with African cultural expressions, internalized racism, or rejection of heritage. Dr. Joy DeGruy, in Post Traumatic Slave Syndrome, writes that internalizing false narratives imposed by oppression perpetuates cycles of trauma. This shame becomes a barrier to fully embracing identity and undermines the ability to honor the sacrifices and contributions of ancestors. Addressing this requires more than acknowledgment—it demands a transformative process of reclaiming history and reinterpreting it as a source of pride and empowerment.

Breaking the silence that perpetuates shame begins with trust in the strength of future generations to bear the truth, trust in the wisdom of ancestors, and trust in the transformative power of confronting history. The Jewish principle of "Never Again," which emphasizes the importance of remembering the Holocaust to prevent its repetition, offers a compelling example of how communities can use painful histories as a foundation for empowerment. By documenting and sharing their experiences, Jewish communities ensure that their history remains a living force for education and resilience. Similarly, African-descended families can trust that sharing their truths, no matter how painful, will strengthen the bridge between generations.

Re-framing narratives of oppression as stories of resilience is an essential part of this healing process. The same history that carries trauma also carries triumph: enslaved Africans preserved their humanity through music, storytelling, and spirituality; civil rights leaders risked their lives for justice; and countless individuals built lives of dignity despite systemic barriers. Educators, cultural leaders, and families play a pivotal role in this transformation. Schools that teach African and African American history empower students to see themselves as inheritors of a continuum of excellence. Cultural institutions that create spaces for storytelling and celebration foster pride in Black identity.

Storytelling, in particular, is a powerful tool for breaking the cycle of shame. When elders share their experiences—whether through spoken word, memoirs, or community gatherings—they provide younger generations with a fuller understanding of their legacy. These stories offer context for both struggles and victories, serving as inspiration and guidance. In this way, storytelling becomes a bridge, connecting the past to the present while ensuring that future generations carry the torch forward. Griots in African culture exemplify this tradition, preserving history and values through oral storytelling. Today, the practice of storytelling continues to be a means of reclaiming and celebrating Blackness, whether through literature, film, or community dialogue.

Rituals and reflective practices also play a crucial role in confronting shame and embracing pride. Pouring libations, commemorating ancestors, and participating in cultural ceremonies allow individuals and communities to honor the past while reaffirming connections to heritage. These acts of remembrance serve as powerful counterweights to narratives of shame, replacing them with a sense of belonging and purpose. They remind us that history is not a burden but a source of strength, resilience, and wisdom.

Ultimately, breaking the silence and transforming shame into pride is a collective responsibility. Families must create safe spaces for intergenerational dialogue, schools must teach history in ways that honor the full humanity of African-descended people, and communities must celebrate their heritage through festivals, art, and activism. These efforts weave a tapestry of trust that strengthens bonds across generations. Confronting shame is not an act of dwelling on the past—it is an act of liberation, a way to break free from the false narratives that have sought to confine us.

By reclaiming history and embracing identity, African-descended people can replace shame with pride and silence with dialogue. Trust in ourselves, our ancestors, and future generations becomes the foundation for a legacy of resilience, empowerment, and collective progress. In doing so, we transform not only how we see our past but also how we shape our future.

The Importance of Oral History and the Written Word

In African societies, griots preserved history, values, and traditions through oral storytelling, ensuring that knowledge passed seamlessly from one generation to the next. These oral traditions provided a lifeline, maintaining identity and continuity even in the face of disruption.

Today, however, oral history alone is insufficient. The written word has become a critical tool for preserving legacy, especially in a climate where erasure and revisionism threaten the truth. Documenting our stories ensures that future generations can access, learn from, and carry them forward.

Dr. Carter G. Woodson, the father of Black history, argued in The Mis-Education of the Negro, "If you can control a man's thinking, you don't have to worry about his actions." Writing our narratives protects our history from manipulation, empowering future generations to build on a foundation of truth.
This dual approach—honoring oral traditions while embracing written records—demonstrates a commitment to trust in action. It proclaims, "We honor the eyes behind us, and we trust the eyes ahead of us to carry this forward."

Generational Silence and Its Impact
Generational silence disrupts the flow of legacy. Elders who lived through Jim Crow or other oppressive systems often chose not to share their stories, hoping to protect their children from the pain of those experiences. While their intentions were loving, this silence left gaps in the collective understanding of history.
Kazemde recalls asking his mother why she hadn't spoken about the horrors of Jim Crow. Her response was simple: "I didn't want you to carry that pain." While her choice was rooted in love, it also created a barrier to fully understanding the strength and resilience she embodied.

Breaking this silence is an act of courage and trust. It involves sharing the truth of our history—the pain, the resilience, and the triumphs—with the next generation, ensuring they understand both the struggles and the strengths that define their legacy.

Reclaiming Pride and Rebuilding Trust
Reclaiming pride in Blackness is vital to rebuilding trust within ourselves and our communities. It begins with rejecting the narratives of shame imposed by oppressive systems and embracing the beauty, strength, and contributions of African-descended people. Marimba Ani, in Yurugu, writes, "We must reconnect with our spiritual and cultural essence to build a future rooted in trust and resilience." This reclamation is not only about personal pride—it is about

fostering a collective culture of empowerment, trust, and unity. By documenting our stories, fostering open dialogue, and celebrating Black excellence, we create a legacy that strengthens bonds across generations. This shared trust forms the foundation of a thriving community, bridging the gaps left by historical trauma and systemic oppression.

Conclusion: Transforming Burdens into Bridges

The burden of shame and silence that has shadowed African-descended communities is not insurmountable—it is an invitation to reclaim and redefine our narrative. The legacies of trauma and systemic oppression do not erase the brilliance, strength, and resilience of our ancestors; they amplify the necessity of telling our stories with pride. Breaking generational silence and confronting imposed shame is an act of liberation, a reclamation of our collective identity and purpose.

This transformation is not merely about confronting the past; it is about shaping the future. By addressing the pain and embracing the triumphs of our history, we plant seeds of pride, resilience, and trust for generations to come. Sharing our truths openly and unapologetically strengthens the bonds within our communities, affirming that we are not alone in this journey. It is through this process that we move from being carriers of burdens to being builders of bridges. The silence of one generation can fracture trust, but the courage to speak can mend it. Trust in ourselves, trust in our collective strength, and trust in the next generation to carry these truths forward are the foundations upon which we build a thriving legacy. As we turn shame into pride and silence into voice, we create a powerful momentum that uplifts our communities and paves the way for a future defined not by the wounds of oppression but by the triumphs of resilience and unity.

REFLECTION QUESTIONS

How have the stories of your ancestors influenced your understanding of trust and legacy?

What steps can you take to preserve and share your family's history? How can oral and written traditions complement each other in building a lasting legacy?

How can breaking generational silence strengthen the bonds between past, present, and future?

What seeds of trust are you planting today for the next generation?

Action Steps

Document Your Family History: Interview elders, record their stories, and preserve them for future generations.

Create a Legacy Journal: Write down your reflections, values, and lessons for the next generation.

Host a Storytelling Night: Invite family or community members to share stories of resilience, love, and trust.

Celebrate Black Excellence: Support initiatives that uplift African-descended communities, fostering pride and unity.

Commit to Learning: Engage with books, documentaries, or events that deepen your understanding of African and African-American history.

Notes

Chapter 8:

Igniting Minds: Trusting Education to Build Communities

"Education is our passport to the future, for tomorrow belongs to those who prepare for it today."

- Malcolm X

Education as Liberation

Education is more than books and lessons. It's trust in action—a bridge between generations, a way of transmitting values, culture, and legacy. For too long, however, African American communities have been asked to trust educational systems that distort our stories, undervalue our children, and disconnect us from our roots.

Dr. Asa G. Hilliard III understood this better than anyone. To him, education was liberation. It was the key to reconnecting our children to their heritage, helping them see their own brilliance, and equipping them to build communities rooted in trust and strength. Hilliard's passion came from his own awakening. As a child, he had believed that his history began with enslavement. But one day, he learned about Africa's great civilizations—empires that rivaled any in the world. "That day changed my life," he said. "I went from thinking I was an accident of history to realizing I was its author."
That realization fueled his life's work. Hilliard spent decades challenging schools to embed Black history and culture into their curricula. "Education," he said, "is a process of transmission. What are we transmitting to our children?" For him, the answer had to be clear: a sense of identity, pride, and purpose.

Dr. Amos Wilson extended Hilliard's vision by addressing the role of identity in education. A psychologist and social theorist, Wilson believed education was never neutral—it either served to liberate or to control. His groundbreaking work, The Developmental Psychology of the Black Child, argued that a child's sense of self was directly tied to their ability to succeed. "If education doesn't prepare our children to sustain and build their communities," Wilson said, "then it's not education at all." He urged educators and families to reclaim the narratives that define our children. To Wilson, trust began with truth: teaching children who they are and helping them see their place in the world.

Dr. Chike Akua took this principle into classrooms and homes. In his book, Education for Transformation, Akua described every child as a "genius waiting to be unlocked." He challenged teachers to create environments where students could see themselves reflected in the curriculum. "If your students can't see themselves in what you teach," Akua often asked, "what are you really teaching them?"

Akua's work underscores the idea that education must be deeply personal. It's not just about academic achievement—it's about belonging. When children trust that their stories matter, they begin to see their potential, and their communities thrive.

While the philosophies of Dr. Hilliard, Dr. Wilson, and Dr. Akua offer a transformative vision for education, their ideas find practical application in a growing movement: the rise of homeschooling and alternative education among African American families. This movement is a modern expression of trust in action, re-imagining education as a path to liberation.

The Rise of Homeschooling and Alternative Education

Over the past two decades, African American families have increasingly turned to homeschooling and alternative education models to provide their children with culturally affirming and academically rigorous learning environments. While the homeschooling movement was historically dominated by white, middle-class families, recent years have seen an explosion of interest among African American families, with the percentage of Black homeschoolings rising from 1.2% in 1999 to an astonishing 16.1% by 2020.
This shift is not just a response to dissatisfaction with traditional schools; it reflects a deeper desire to reclaim control over the narratives and values transmitted to children. In many mainstream schools, African American history is marginalized, and Black students are disproportionately subjected to punitive discipline and low expectations. Homeschooling offers a way to counter these systemic inequities by creating environments where children are valued, empowered, and seen.

The Power of Choice

The rise of homeschooling is rooted in the principle of choice—the choice to design an education that meets the unique needs of African American children. Parents who choose homeschooling often cite three key factors:

Cultural Affirmation: Many Black families are frustrated by the Euro-centric focus of public school curricula, which often fails to reflect the histories, achievements, and contributions of African-descended people. Homeschooling allows families to center African and African American history, ensuring that children grow up with a strong sense of identity and pride.

Academic Rigor: Homeschooling provides the flexibility to tailor lessons to a child's interests and strengths, often leading to higher academic achievement. Research shows that home-schooled students consistently outperform their public school peers on standardized tests, with African American homeschoolers achieving particularly impressive results.

Emotional Safety: For many Black parents, traditional schools are seen as unsafe spaces where their children are at risk of being criminalized or undervalued. Homeschooling offers a sanctuary where children can learn free from racial bias and microaggressions.

The Data Speaks

Category	Average Percentile Score
Homeschool Students	85%
Public School Students	60

This achievement gap demonstrates the potential of culturally affirming and personalized education to unlock the brilliance of Black children.

Alternative Models of Education

The rise of homeschooling has also inspired the growth of alternative education models, such as African-centered schools and micro-schools. These institutions combine the flexibility of homeschooling with the structure of traditional schooling, creating environments where children can thrive both academically and culturally. African-centered schools, in particular, are grounded in the principles of Sankofa, the Adinkra symbol meaning "go back and fetch it." These schools emphasize the importance of reclaiming African traditions and applying them to contemporary challenges. Students learn not only math and science but also cultural pride, community responsibility, and leadership skills.

Micro-schools, which are small, community-based learning environments, have also gained traction among Black families. These schools often operate with fewer than 50 students and focus on personalized learning and strong teacher-student relationships. Because

of their size and flexibility, micro-schools can quickly adapt curricula to address the specific needs and interests of their students.
While homeschooling and alternative education are reclaiming agency over learning, the fight for equitable public education continues. Efforts to incorporate culturally responsive teaching, anti-bias training for educators, and more inclusive curricula are gaining traction, ensuring that public schools reflect the diversity of their students. These parallel efforts demonstrate the dual approach of community empowerment and systemic advocacy, bridging the work of families, educators, and policymakers.

The growth of homeschooling and alternative education is not just about academics—it is a profound act of trust. Families are choosing to reclaim control over their children's futures, creating environments where trust in identity, culture, and community are central. This trust forms the foundation of a movement that goes beyond individual families to inspire systemic change.

A Movement Rooted in Trust

The rise of homeschooling and alternative education among African Americans is far more than a critique of traditional schooling; it is a bold and transformative declaration of trust. At its core, this movement is rooted in trust in the brilliance of Black children, the enduring strength of Black families, and the collective power of Black communities to design educational systems that honor identity, foster achievement, and inspire self-determination.

Trust in the Brilliance of Black Children

At the heart of this movement is an unshakable belief in the potential of Black children. For too long, mainstream educational systems have underestimated and undervalued their capabilities, perpetuating low expectations and stifling their growth. Homeschooling and alternative education allow families to reject these narratives and create spaces where children are celebrated for their unique talents, intelligence, and creativity.

Dr. Amos Wilson, in The Developmental Psychology of the Black Child, underscored the critical connection between education and identity. "If a child is to develop fully, they must be rooted in an education that reflects their heritage and builds their confidence." Trust in the brilliance of Black children means recognizing their capacity to excel when nurtured in environments that affirm their worth and potential.

Trust in the Power of Community

The movement toward homeschooling is not an isolated phenomenon—it is deeply communal. Black families have long understood the importance of collective responsibility in raising and educating children. This ethos is embodied in the proverb, "It takes a village to raise a child." Homeschooling families often form co-ops, learning pods, and support networks that mirror the communal spirit of African traditions, ensuring that no family has to navigate this journey alone.

Dr. Cheryl Fields-Smith's research highlights the collaborative nature of Black homeschooling communities, where families pool resources, share expertise, and organize joint learning experiences. "Black homeschooling," she writes, "is a modern manifestation of mutual aid, a testament to the resilience and ingenuity of our communities."

A Personal Reflection on Trust and Education

I saw this power of education and trust firsthand during a recent conversation with my granddaughter. She was in her senior year of high school, attending a majority-white school in southeast Georgia. For years, I had encouraged her to read about our history, to explore her heritage. But one day, she revealed just how much the narratives she was absorbing in school had shaped her thinking. We were talking about lineage, and when I mentioned Africa, she pushed back. "I don't want anything to do with Africa," she said. "They're backwards, and they sold us into slavery."

Her words stung. They reminded me of the images I saw as a child—those Tarzan movies that depicted Africans as primitive and uncivilized. I had encountered so many others in my life who felt ashamed of being connected to Africa, upset about the idea that Africans had sold their own people into bondage.

I decided to ask her a question. "If someone came into your house," I said, "captured and kidnapped your family, tortured you with rifles and knives, and then demanded you set up another household for capture, or risk the lives of your loved ones—what would you do?"

She paused, thinking.

"Some people might choose to die," I continued, "and I'm sure some did. But others might choose to protect their families, even if it meant betraying others. Now tell me, who is the perpetrator, and who is the victim?"

For the first time, she began to question the narrative she'd been taught. I reminded her that she can't trust someone else to define who she is or where she comes from. "Google is a wonderful thing," I told her. "Search for cityscapes in Africa. Look beyond what you've been told. And read—like I've been telling you."

That conversation was a turning point. She's now reading the books I suggest to her, exploring stories of African brilliance and resilience that weren't taught in her school. She's beginning to understand that the history she was handed doesn't define her—it's just one version of a much larger truth.

The Ripple Effect

What struck me most about my conversation with my granddaughter wasn't just her change in perspective—it was the ripple effect. When one person reclaims their story, it doesn't stop with them. It spreads to their family, their friends, and their community, planting seeds of curiosity and pride that grow into something greater.

This ripple effect is not just a possibility—it's happening. From the rise of homeschooling movements to the creation of African-centered schools, Black families and communities are rejecting harmful narratives and building systems that reflect their values and aspirations. These efforts are planting the seeds of a new legacy, one rooted in trust, pride, and purpose.

The impact of these efforts can also be seen in broader community initiatives. For example, grassroots organizations like Freedom Schools and cultural centers are partnering with families to create spaces where children can explore their heritage. These organizations often influence local education policies, advocating for inclusive curricula, equitable funding, and professional development for teachers in cultural competency.

Policy reform, when combined with community-led efforts, amplifies the ripple effect. By demonstrating the effectiveness of culturally affirming education models, homeschooling families and alternative schools challenge mainstream systems to adopt practices that reflect the diversity and brilliance of their students. The ripple effect extends beyond individual families, inspiring systemic change that benefits entire communities.

When we invest in education that centers our children's history, culture, and potential, we create generations of leaders and change makers. The ripple effect is a testament to the power of trusting our children, trusting our communities, and trusting our ability to shape the world around us.

The ripple effect reminds us that reclaiming education is not just a personal journey—it is a communal responsibility. As individuals transform their understanding of history and identity, they lay the groundwork for collective empowerment. This ripple leads to a larger vision of education as liberation, a vision that must guide our actions moving forward.

Education as Liberation

Education is not just a tool for personal success—it is the foundation of community empowerment and transformation. It is the vessel through which values, culture, and legacy are transmitted across generations. When we trust in the brilliance of our children, the strength of our communities, and the power of our stories, we create an education system that liberates rather than limits.
Trust in education is about more than academics—it is about shaping identity, inspiring confidence, and nurturing potential. It is about ensuring that every child understands not just where they come from, but also where they are capable of going. This trust begins with reclaiming our history, centering our narratives, and teaching our children to see themselves as part of a legacy of resilience and excellence.

Dr. Asa G. Hilliard III described education as a "process of transmission." The question he posed to educators and parents alike was simple but profound: What are we transmitting to our children? Are we transmitting pride, self-worth, and the knowledge of their boundless potential? Or are we allowing distorted narratives to undermine their sense of identity and possibility? The answer to these questions determines the trajectory of not just individuals but entire communities.

Education as liberation also requires an intergenerational lens. Elders, who hold the wisdom of lived experience, are vital in transmitting trust and resilience to younger generations. By sharing their stories and struggles, they bridge gaps in understanding, ensuring that the lessons of the past guide the progress of the future. Children, in turn, inspire elders with their bold visions and untapped potential, creating a cycle of mutual trust and empowerment.

The spiritual dimension of education cannot be overlooked. Historically, African and African American traditions wove spirituality into learning as a source of inspiration and connection. From the communal rituals of African villages to the hymns of the Black Church, education was both a spiritual and intellectual pursuit. By integrating these elements, we create a more holistic approach to learning, one that nurtures the soul as much as the mind.

Policy reform must accompany these grassroots efforts. Advocacy for equitable funding, inclusion of African-centered curricula, and anti-bias training for educators ensures that systemic barriers do not undo the progress made by families and communities. By working both within and outside the system, we create a comprehensive strategy for educational liberation.

Imagine a world where every Black child grows up knowing their worth, their history, and their potential. A world where education reflects the rich tapestry of African and African American contributions to human history. A world where classrooms are spaces of empowerment, not alienation—where learning is an act of liberation. This is the vision we must work toward—a vision where trust and education converge to create thriving communities, resilient families, and confident, capable leaders. It is not a distant ideal but a tangible goal, one that begins with the choices we make today. By investing in culturally affirming education, supporting alternative models like homeschooling and micro-schools, and reclaiming our narratives, we lay the foundation for a future of pride, purpose, and possibility.

Dr. Chike Akua reminds us that education is the blueprint for building communities. "When we control the narrative, we control the future," he wrote. This truth underscores the urgency of the work ahead. The education we provide today will shape the leaders, innovators, and change makers of tomorrow.

As we move forward, let us remember that education is not simply about knowledge—it is about liberation. It is about freeing our minds, restoring our spirits, and empowering our communities. Let us embrace the responsibility of shaping an education system that reflects the best of who we are and who we aspire to be.

The future belongs to those who trust in the power of education to transform lives and communities. Let us ensure that trust is rooted in love, pride, and a commitment to excellence. This is how we honor our ancestors, uplift our children, and build a legacy of liberation for generations to come.

REFLECTION QUESTIONS

How has education shaped your understanding of your identity and heritage?

What role does trust play in how you approach learning and teaching in your community?

How can homeschooling, alternative education, or community-led education initiatives benefit your family or neighborhood?

Action Steps

Explore local or virtual African-centered educational programs or resources to supplement your family's learning.

Share one book, article, or documentary about African or African American history with someone in your community.

Join or support a homeschooling co-op, learning pod, or micro-school that reflects your values and priorities.

Create a family tradition of discussing and documenting your own family history and cultural roots.

Notes

Chapter 9

Trust & Economic Equity

"The economic empowerment of our people must rest upon a foundation of self-respect, cultural integrity, and mutual trust."

– Dr. John Henrik Clarke

The Role of Trust and Spirituality in Economic Equity

Economic equity transcends the simple accumulation of wealth; it embodies the principles of opportunity, access, and the ability to thrive in systems that honor fairness, justice, and shared prosperity. It is not merely about closing gaps or leveling playing fields; it is about creating transformative conditions where individuals and communities can flourish holistically—socially, culturally, and spiritually.

For Black communities, the journey toward economic equity has been an odyssey of resilience and innovation. Despite systemic barriers, the unshakable spirit of Black people has turned challenges into opportunities, building a legacy of creativity, enterprise, and self-determination. At the heart of this journey lies trust—not just in external systems, which have historically failed Black communities, but in ourselves, our families, and the collective strength of our communities. This trust is more than an interpersonal virtue; it is the backbone of spiritual and economic empowerment, a force that fuels collective progress.

When Black people engage in any endeavor, we bring "that 'it' factor"—a powerful blend of creativity, resilience, and spiritual energy that transforms the ordinary into the extraordinary. This intangible quality has long been a hallmark of Black excellence, manifesting in fields as diverse as art, business, politics, and activism. The spiritual dimension of this energy is its most profound attribute: an unseen force that ignites potential and drives greatness. Yet, for this energy to flourish, it must be rooted in trust and channeled through thoughtful, strategic action.

Trust serves as the foundation for sustainable progress. It binds communities, fosters collaboration, and creates the stability necessary for long-term growth. Spirituality, in turn, provides the guiding principles that shape how trust is cultivated and applied. Within African and African-descended traditions, the spiritual and material worlds are not separate but deeply interconnected. This worldview positions economic equity not as an isolated pursuit but as an integral part of the broader struggle for justice, dignity, and collective well-being.

As we embark on this exploration of trust, spirituality, and economic equity, we are reminded that the journey is as much about internal transformation as it is about external outcomes. This chapter delves into the historical and systemic challenges that have shaped

Black economic experiences, shedding light on the internal dynamics of resilience and resourcefulness that have allowed communities to endure and thrive. From the Great Migration to the entrepreneurial spirit of Greenwood, and from systemic barriers to contemporary movements for economic justice, we will uncover the enduring lessons that can guide us toward collective success.

This chapter challenges us to re-imagine economic equity not as a distant goal but as a present possibility. It invites us to consider the profound role of trust and spirituality in shaping our collective path forward. As we weave together historical insights, contemporary realities, and a vision for the future, we are called to embrace trust as both a principle and a practice—a foundation upon which a more equitable and spiritually aligned world can be built.

The Great Migration: A Spiritual and Economic Journey

The Great Migration, spanning from 1916 to 1970, was one of the most significant movements of African Americans in U.S. history. Millions left the rural South for northern cities like Chicago, Detroit, New York City, and Philadelphia, seeking industrial jobs and escaping the systemic racism of Jim Crow.

This migration was not just a physical journey—it was a spiritual one. Black families carried with them the hopes and dreams of a better future, as well as the cultural and spiritual practices that would sustain them in unfamiliar environments. The energy and resilience they brought to northern cities transformed these urban centers into vibrant hubs of Black culture and economic activity.

The following table illustrates the dramatic growth of Black populations in northern cities during this period:

City	Population Growth (in thousands)
New York City	65
Chicago	148
Detroit	611
Philadelphia	58
Baltimore	31
Cleveland	57
St. Louis	37
Newark	25

This growth fueled the rise of the Black middle class, with opportunities in factories, shipyards, and steel mills. Black churches, businesses, and cultural institutions flourished, creating communities that were both economically and spiritually rich.

The Breakdown of Community Trust

Despite the initial promise of the Great Migration, systemic racism reasserted itself in new and insidious ways:
Housing Discrimination: Redlining and discriminatory lending practices confined Black families to overcrowded neighborhoods with substandard housing.

Healthcare Inequities: Lack of access to adequate healthcare left Black communities vulnerable to preventable illnesses.
Over-Policing: Discriminatory law enforcement practices created a climate of fear and mistrust.

These external forces eroded the trust that had sustained Black communities, but internal dynamics also played a role. As integration opened new opportunities, Black-owned businesses struggled to compete with corporate chains. Many Black families, swayed by the perception that "their ice was colder," turned away from their own communities' enterprises.

The following table highlights the disparity between Black-owned and white-owned businesses in 1960:

Business Type	Number of Businesses
Black-Owned Businesses	50,000
White-Owned Businesses	3,500,000

This loss of trust in Black businesses marked a turning point, as economic resources began flowing outward rather than circulating within the community.

Greenwood and the Spirit of Excellence

The story of Greenwood, often referred to as Black Wall Street, stands as a monumental testament to Black economic excellence and ingenuity. It was more than a neighborhood; it was a thriving ecosystem of entrepreneurship, cultural pride, and communal trust. Located in Tulsa, Oklahoma, Greenwood flourished in the early 20th century, fueled by the collective ambition and resilience of its Black residents. At its peak, Greenwood was home to bustling businesses, schools, churches, and cultural institutions, all owned and operated by Black entrepreneurs and supported by a community committed to mutual success.

Greenwood's success was not accidental. It was the result of deliberate trust-building, collaboration, and a shared vision of self-reliance and prosperity. Residents understood the importance of circulating wealth within their community, creating a robust economic infrastructure that allowed them to thrive despite the pervasive racism and segregation of the time. It was a place where Black professionals—doctors, lawyers, teachers, and entrepreneurs—could flourish, and where families could build a future grounded in dignity and opportunity.

However, Greenwood's achievements were not immune to the forces of systemic racism and violence that sought to dismantle Black progress across the United States. In 1921, the community was brutally attacked during the Tulsa Race Massacre, one of the most devastating incidents of racial violence in American history. A white mob, incited by false accusations and fueled by racial hatred, descended on Greenwood, killing hundreds, destroying homes and businesses, and leaving thousands of residents homeless. The destruction was swift and merciless, erasing decades of hard work and ambition in a matter of hours.

The aftermath of the massacre was equally devastating. Insurance companies refused to compensate victims for their losses, and local and federal governments offered no support for rebuilding. The systemic barriers that had long oppressed Black communities now ensured that Greenwood's recovery would be nearly impossible. Yet, even in the face of this profound injustice, the spirit of Greenwood did not die. Its legacy endures as a symbol of what is possible when trust, collaboration, and a shared vision come together.
Greenwood challenges us to reflect on the resilience and ingenuity of Black communities in the face of unimaginable adversity. It is a reminder of the heights that can be reached when trust is cultivated and nurtured within a community. At the same time, it serves as a stark warning of the fragility of progress in the absence of systemic

protections and accountability. Greenwood forces us to confront the question: How do we reclaim this spirit of excellence and ensure it is not extinguished again?

Reclaiming the spirit of Greenwood begins with recognizing the value of trust as the foundation of collective success. Trust must be rebuilt within Black communities and extended into the systems and institutions that shape economic opportunities. This involves not only fostering collaboration and self-reliance but also addressing the systemic inequities that continue to undermine Black progress. It means advocating for policies that protect Black entrepreneurs and communities, creating access to capital and resources, and ensuring that the mistakes of the past are not repeated.

To honor the legacy of Greenwood, we must also embrace the lessons of resilience and vision that defined its success. Greenwood thrived because its residents believed in their ability to create a self-sufficient community rooted in dignity and opportunity. Today, we can draw inspiration from this example by supporting Black-owned businesses, investing in community-based initiatives, and building networks of collaboration that reflect the values of trust and mutual upliftment.

Greenwood is not just a story of what was lost; it is a story of what can be achieved when trust and excellence are at the forefront. It reminds us that Black economic success is not only possible but inevitable when communities come together with purpose and determination. By reclaiming this spirit and building on its legacy, we can create a future that honors Greenwood's vision while forging new pathways for equity and prosperity.

As we reflect on Greenwood's history, we must carry forward its lessons and confront its challenges with clarity and purpose. The spirit of Greenwood lives on in every Black entrepreneur, every community collaboration, and every effort to build a more equitable world. Let us not only rebuild but re-imagine what is possible, drawing strength from Greenwood's example to create a future where economic excellence is not the exception but the rule.

The Intersection of Economics and Politics

Economic equity does not exist in a vacuum—it is deeply intertwined with the political systems that define access, opportunity, and progress. As Professor James Small profoundly stated, "Politics is the management of our economy." This relationship underscores the critical role political systems play in shaping the conditions under which businesses and communities either thrive or struggle. Whether through access to resources, infrastructure development, or the protections provided to entrepreneurs and workers, politics weaves itself into the very fabric of economic equity.

In Black communities, this connection has been particularly pronounced. Historical barriers such as redlining, discriminatory lending practices, and underfunded public resources have long illustrated how political systems can both inhibit and enable economic opportunity. To counteract these systemic challenges, Black communities have often turned to political engagement as a strategy to create economic pathways. This begins not at the federal level, where sweeping policies may feel distant, but locally—where city councils, school boards, and local governments have a direct impact on daily life. Local elections, zoning decisions, and municipal investments can significantly influence whether Black businesses receive the resources and support they need to succeed.

Creating these smoother pathways for Black enterprises requires deliberate action. Advocacy for equitable lending practices and access to capital is one such step. Black entrepreneurs often face disproportionately high rejection rates when seeking business loans, which stifles growth and limits opportunities for innovation. By lobbying for fair lending policies and fostering community-driven banking institutions, Black communities can carve out financial opportunities that serve their specific needs. Supporting candidates and policies that prioritize infrastructure and community investment is equally vital. Roads, utilities, and technology access may seem like background factors, but they are the backbone of thriving businesses. A store or service cannot succeed if its community lacks the means to access it. Building coalitions that amplify the voices of Black entrepreneurs and workers further strengthens these efforts, ensuring that those who understand the unique challenges of Black enterprise are actively shaping the solutions.

Understanding this intersection between economics and politics is not just a theoretical exercise; it is a fundamental step in creating systems of trust and equity. Political engagement, when grounded in collective action, becomes a powerful tool to dismantle systemic barriers and foster economic environments where all can flourish.

This work calls for a strategic understanding of policy, persistent advocacy, and the courage to demand better from those in positions of power. It also requires unity—a shared commitment among individuals and communities to recognize the transformative potential of their combined voices and votes.

Intergenerational Wisdom and Trust

Economic equity is not solely a contemporary issue. Its roots and future depend on intergenerational wisdom and trust. Beyond addressing present challenges, building a legacy of equity involves intentional planning for the prosperity of future generations. The concept of economic equity must extend beyond immediate outcomes, focusing on long-term sustainability through the transmission of knowledge, resources, and values.

Teaching the next generation is an essential act of trust and empowerment. Parents, elders, and mentors play pivotal roles in sharing their experiences and wisdom, ensuring that young people understand not only the value of economic equity, but also the principles of trust and collaboration that underpin it. These lessons, grounded in lived experiences, offer a road map for navigating and overcoming systemic obstacles.

Oral and written histories both hold essential places in this legacy-building process. Oral traditions, which have long been a cornerstone of Black cultural preservation, carry the voices of ancestors, sharing stories of resilience, triumph, and the strategies that sustained communities through centuries of adversity. These spoken accounts are invaluable, connecting each generation to its roots and instilling a sense of identity and purpose. However, the written word also has a critical role. Documenting these histories ensures that they endure beyond memory, providing a tangible record that can be studied, referenced, and built upon. Books, articles, and personal memoirs serve as enduring legacies, bridging the gap between generations and offering a foundation for future progress.

Intergenerational wisdom is more than a transfer of knowledge; it is an act of trust. Elders must trust that the younger generation will honor their sacrifices and carry their vision forward. In turn, the younger generation must trust the guidance and insights of those who came before, while also bringing fresh perspectives to adapt to an ever-changing world. This mutual trust fosters a dynamic exchange, where tradition and innovation coexist, ensuring that economic equity is not only achieved but also sustained. By embracing this intergenerational collaboration, Black communities can build a foundation of prosperity that respects the past, empowers the present, and secures the future.

Call to Action: Building a New Vision

The path forward requires us to reclaim the principles that once enabled Black communities to thrive, weaving trust, preparation, and collective success into the fabric of our economic and social system. These values are not relics of the past; they are enduring truths that have powered resilience and creativity even in the face of systemic challenges. To build a new vision for economic equity and communal strength, we must turn these principles into actionable strategies that not only honor our history, but also lay the foundation for a prosperous future.

One of the most immediate and impactful ways to move forward is by supporting Black-owned businesses. These enterprises are not just economic entities; they are cultural hubs and symbols of self-determination. By consciously choosing to shop at and invest in Black-owned businesses, we keep economic resources circulating within our communities, strengthening the foundation for generational wealth. The multiplying effect of supporting local Black businesses extends beyond individual transactions. It contributes to job creation, fosters economic independence, and reinforces a sense of pride and ownership within the community. Historical models like the Greenwood District in Tulsa, often referred to as Black Wall Street, demonstrate the power of collective investment in Black enterprises. Despite its tragic destruction, Greenwood remains a testament to the economic potential that emerges when resources are concentrated and reinvested within the community.

Supporting Black-owned businesses also requires a shift in mindset—an intentional commitment to value and uplift our own enterprises. Overcoming internalized biases that equate quality with proximity to whiteness is a necessary step in this process. It is about trusting and believing in the excellence that Black entrepreneurs bring to their industries, whether it is in technology, arts, retail, or professional services. Efforts like Buy Black initiatives, marketplaces, and apps dedicated to connecting consumers with Black businesses are tools that make this commitment more accessible. By participating in these movements, we strengthen the economic ecosystem that sustains our communities and aligns with the principles of equity and empowerment.

Equally important is the need to build networks of collaboration that connect individuals, businesses, and institutions. Trust is the lifeblood of collaboration, enabling diverse stakeholders to work together toward mutual success. These networks are not only about pooling resources, but also about fostering innovation through shared ideas and collective problem-solving. For instance, cooperative economic models, such as those seen in African and Caribbean communities, provide a framework for mutual support and shared benefit. These models emphasize trust and accountability, creating a safety net for participants while driving collective progress. Today, initiatives like Black cooperative banks and community investment funds are modern iterations of these age-old principles, illustrating how collaboration can be adapted to address contemporary challenges.

Building such networks also means breaking down silos between sectors. Entrepreneurs, educators, policymakers, and community leaders must find ways to work together, recognizing that the challenges facing Black communities are interconnected. For example, the success of a Black-owned grocery store depends not only on consumer support, but also on access to affordable transportation, equitable zoning laws, and partnerships with local farmers. Collaboration among these stakeholders ensures that the systems surrounding the business are just as robust as the business itself. By fostering these interconnected networks, we create an environment where success becomes a shared endeavor rather than an individual achievement.

Preparation is the third pillar of this call to action, serving as both a mindset and a strategy. Preparation is an act of empowerment, equipping individuals and communities to anticipate challenges and navigate uncertainty with confidence. It begins with understanding the landscape—analyzing market trends, identifying potential barriers, and seeking out opportunities for growth. But preparation goes beyond analysis; it requires creating contingency plans and building systems of resilience that can weather economic fluctuations or unexpected obstacles.

Historically, preparation has been a cornerstone of Black resilience. From the self-sufficient farming communities that arose during Reconstruction to the organized boycotts of the Civil Rights Movement, strategic planning has always been integral to Black survival and progress. Today, this principle can be applied through initiatives like financial literacy programs, which empower individuals to manage resources effectively and make informed decisions. Additionally, mentorship programs that pair experienced business leaders with aspiring entrepreneurs provide invaluable guidance, helping to mitigate risks and build confidence. These efforts ensure that preparation is not left to chance, but is woven into the fabric of community-building efforts.

Preparation also involves institutional planning. Communities must develop mechanisms for collective resilience, such as community land trusts that safeguard housing affordability or cooperative food systems that ensure access to healthy, affordable meals. These structures not only address immediate needs but also lay the groundwork for long-term sustainability. Strategic preparation at the institutional level sends a clear message: we are not merely reacting to external pressures but proactively shaping our future.

Ultimately, building a new vision requires integrating these principles—support for Black-owned businesses, collaborative networks, and strategic preparation—into a unified framework for action. This vision is not just about economic growth; it is about cultivating a sense of collective empowerment and responsibility. It is about trusting one another and believing in the transformative potential of unity and intentionality. By reclaiming the principles that have always sustained us, we can create a future that reflects the strength, resilience, and creativity of our communities.

Conclusion: Trust, Love, and Spiritual Excellence

The lessons of the Great Migration, the triumphs and trials of Greenwood, and the enduring systemic challenges faced by Black communities all converge on a profound and unchanging truth: economic equity begins with trust, love, and strategic planning. These three pillars are not merely abstract ideals; they are the foundational principles that have guided our communities through eras of adversity and toward moments of triumph. They remind us that progress is not about survival alone—it is about thriving in ways that honor our history and propel us into a future defined by possibility.

When Black people engage in any endeavor, we bring with us "that 'it' factor"—a distinctive blend of spiritual and cultural energy that transforms the ordinary into the extraordinary. This intangible quality, deeply rooted in our collective history, has been the driving force behind our artistic innovations, entrepreneurial ventures, and social movements. It is the essence of our resilience, creativity, and excellence. But this energy cannot fully flourish without a foundation of trust. Trust is what binds our communities, fortifies our relationships, and sustains our collective dreams in the face of systemic challenges. It is the connective tissue that transforms individual efforts into a shared vision for progress.

Love is the second pillar, equally essential in building a future that reflects our values. Love for our heritage, our people, and our communities is what inspires us to push beyond the barriers imposed by systemic inequities. This love is not passive or sentimental—it is an active force that demands commitment, accountability, and care. Love drives us to uplift one another, to nurture the next generation, and to create spaces of healing and belonging. It is the wellspring of our resilience, the force that ensures we do not falter when the path ahead is uncertain. Love is what transforms trust into action, infusing our strategic efforts with purpose and meaning.

Strategic planning is the third and final pillar, the practical framework that allows trust and love to manifest in tangible ways. Without strategy, even the most inspired efforts risk being scattered and unsustainable. Strategic planning is what turns dreams into blueprints, aspirations into achievements. It requires foresight, preparation, and a willingness to adapt to changing circumstances. History offers us countless examples of how strategic planning has been a cornerstone of Black resilience—from the organized boycotts of the Civil Rights Movement to the self-sufficient farming communities that emerged after Reconstruction. Today, the principles of strategic planning remain as relevant as ever, guiding us to build systems that are not only equitable but also enduring.

The intersection of these three pillars—trust, love, and strategic planning—provides the foundation for re-imagining what is possible. We are not tasked with simply rebuilding what has been lost. Instead, we are called to dream bigger, to envision a future that surpasses the limitations of the past. This requires a fundamental shift in how we see ourselves and our communities. It means rejecting narratives of scarcity and embracing a mindset of abundance, where the success of one is seen as the success of all. It means creating systems that reflect our highest values, systems that are inclusive, equitable, and sustainable.

To re-imagine what is possible, we must also honor the lessons of those who came before us. The resilience of our ancestors, the sacrifices they made, and the wisdom they passed down are the bedrock upon which we stand. Their stories remind us that progress is neither easy, nor linear, but it is always within reach when we approach it with intention and unity. The spirit of Greenwood, the determination of the Great Migration, and the countless acts of everyday heroism in our communities provide us with a road map for the work ahead. They teach us that trust, love, and strategy are not just tools for survival—they are the keys to liberation.

The time to act is now. As we look to the future, let us ground ourselves in trust, guided by love and fortified by strategic planning. Let us embrace the challenges before us as opportunities to demonstrate our resilience and creativity. Let us not merely rebuild but re-imagine what our communities can become. By doing so, we honor the legacy of those who paved the way and create a foundation upon which future generations can thrive.

The journey toward economic equity is not a destination but an ongoing process—a collective effort that requires each of us to contribute in our own unique way. Together, we can build a future that reflects the best of who we are and what we aspire to be. Let us move forward with clarity, purpose, and a steadfast commitment to trust, love, and spiritual excellence, knowing that the work we do today will shape the possibilities of tomorrow.

REFLECTION QUESTIONS

As we reflect on economic equity, consider these guiding questions: How can you support and invest in Black-owned businesses in your community?

What political actions can you take to advocate for economic equity?

How can intergenerational mentorship strengthen the economic foundation of Black communities?

Action Steps

To translate these principles into practice, consider the following steps as starting points:

Identify and support Black-owned businesses in your area.

Advocate for local policies that address systemic economic inequities.

Mentor young entrepreneurs or community leaders, sharing your knowledge and resources.

Notes

Chapter 10

Trust in Leadership & Governance

"Power at its best is love implementing the demands of justice, and justice at its best is power correcting everything that stands against love."

– Dr. Martin Luther King Jr

Leadership as Service

Leadership is not about power or control—it is about service. True leadership emerges from a commitment to the well-being of others and a desire to create meaningful change. It is rooted in trust, accountability, and shared responsibility. Without trust, leadership falters; without accountability, governance crumbles.

This chapter explores the relationship between trust and leadership, highlighting the qualities of trustworthy leaders, the importance of grassroots movements, and the role of governance in shaping a just and equitable society. At its core, effective leadership is about elevating the voices of those you serve, understanding their needs, and working collectively to meet them.

Chokwe Lumumba, former mayor of Jackson, Mississippi, exemplified this philosophy of leadership as service. Before he ever stepped into political office, he was a grassroots organizer and civil rights attorney who dedicated his life to empowering Black communities. Lumumba's work was grounded in the belief that governance should reflect the will and needs of the people, not the ambitions of those in power. His approach to leadership emphasized collaboration, trust, and accountability, serving as a blueprint for what is possible when leadership emerges from the people rather than being imposed upon them.

Dr. Chike Akua, a renowned educator and leadership strategist, adds another dimension to this discussion. "Leadership is more than a title—it is a responsibility to uplift, empower, and inspire others," he says. Dr. Akua's work in transforming educational spaces and mentoring leaders underscores the transformative power of leadership rooted in trust, cultural awareness, and service. His insights remind us that leadership begins not with a position, but with a purpose.

Leadership as a Catalyst for Trust

Trustworthy leadership inspires confidence, fosters collaboration, and empowers communities. It is built on transparency, accountability, and a genuine commitment to the collective good. Leaders who embody these qualities create environments where trust can thrive, enabling communities to overcome challenges and seize opportunities.

The legacy of Fannie Lou Hamer offers a powerful example of

trust as a cornerstone of leadership. Hamer's work in the Mississippi Freedom Democratic Party exemplified courage, transparency, and accountability. She stood against systemic oppression, articulating the needs of marginalized communities with honesty and integrity. Her leadership inspired trust not only within her community but also on a national stage, demonstrating the transformative power of grassroots leadership.

Another example of leadership rooted in trust is the role of the Southern Tenant Farmers Union (STFU) during the 1930s. Amid extreme racial and economic inequality, this multiracial coalition of sharecroppers and tenant farmers organized to demand fair wages and equitable treatment. The union's leaders, Black and white alike, demonstrated transparency and accountability in their advocacy, earning the trust of their members. This trust enabled them to mobilize marginalized communities, challenge systemic injustices, and push for legislative reforms.

Transparency, honesty, and accountability are not abstract ideals—they are the bedrock of leadership that empowers. Leaders like Hamer and organizations like the STFU remind us that trust is earned through consistent action and a steadfast commitment to serving the collective good.

Grassroots Movements: Leadership from the Ground Up
True leadership often emerges from the grassroots, where individuals and communities come together to address shared challenges and advocate for change. Grassroots movements demonstrate the power of collective action and the importance of trust in achieving shared goals.

Consider the legacy of the Highlander Research and Education Center, a training ground for civil rights leaders such as Rosa Parks and Septima Clark. The Highlander Center embodied the principles of grassroots leadership, prioritizing collaboration, education, and empowerment. By equipping individuals with the tools and knowledge to advocate for justice, the center fostered trust and solidarity among diverse communities.

The example of the Brotherhood of Sleeping Car Porters further underscores the potential of grassroots leadership. Under the guidance of A. Philip Randolph, the union became a catalyst for economic and social progress, advocating for better wages and working conditions for Black workers. The union's leadership built trust by centering the voices of its members, demonstrating that grassroots movements are a powerful engine for change.

Grassroots efforts remind us that leadership is not confined to elected officials or formal titles. It is about individuals and communities taking responsibility for their collective future, advocating for justice, and building systems that reflect their values.

Governance and Economic Equity

Leadership and governance are inextricably linked to economic equity. As Professor James Small states, "Politics is the management system of our economy." Governance shapes the distribution of resources, the creation of opportunities, and the systems that impact daily life. Trust in governance is essential for fostering economic equity and ensuring that all individuals have access to the resources they need to thrive.

Equitable Resource Allocation: Trustworthy governance prioritizes the equitable distribution of resources, addressing disparities and creating opportunities for marginalized communities.
Community Engagement: Governance that involves community members in decision-making processes builds trust and ensures that policies reflect the needs and priorities of the people they serve.
Transparency in Policy Implementation: Trust is built when governance processes are transparent, ensuring that policies are implemented fairly and effectively.

Economic equity is not a theoretical concept—it is a lived experience. When governance fails to prioritize equity, communities suffer. But when leaders are committed to fairness, opportunity, and justice, they create the conditions for individuals and communities to thrive.

Conclusion: Leadership Rooted in Trust

Trust is the foundation of effective leadership and governance. It is the thread that weaves communities together, the bridge that connects leaders to those they serve, and the anchor that grounds governance in equity and justice. Without trust, leadership is hollow, and governance becomes a mechanism of oppression rather than a tool for progress. Leaders who prioritize trust create environments where collaboration, accountability, and resilience thrive, forging pathways for communities to overcome challenges and achieve meaningful change.

Leadership rooted in trust is not about power—it is about service. This ethos is exemplified by leaders who see their role as an opportunity to uplift others, inspire action, and build systems that reflect the collective good. True leadership requires a commitment to equity, an unwavering dedication to accountability, and a willingness to stand in solidarity with the communities one serves. Leaders like Chokwe Lumumba, Fannie Lou Hamer, and A. Philip Randolph understood that trust is not something granted lightly—it is earned through transparency, consistency, and courage.

At its core, trust in leadership is about connection. It is the ability to listen deeply to the needs of others, to prioritize their well-being over personal ambition, and to create a shared vision that reflects the collective aspirations of the community. Effective leadership fosters a sense of belonging, reminding individuals that their voices matter and that their contributions are valued. This connection is not a one-way street—it is a reciprocal relationship where leaders and communities work together to create systems of mutual accountability and shared success.

The story of the Southern Tenant Farmers Union illustrates this reciprocity. By centering the voices of its members and prioritizing their needs, the union built a foundation of trust that empowered individuals to advocate for their rights. Similarly, the grassroots efforts of the Highlander Research and Education Center demonstrate how leadership rooted in trust can catalyze transformative change. These examples remind us that leadership is not confined to titles or positions—it is about taking responsibility for the well-being of others and creating systems that reflect our highest ideals.

Trust also plays a critical role in governance. As Professor James Small aptly noted, "Politics is the management system of our economy." Governance is not just about policies and procedures—it is about the values that guide decision-making and the systems that distribute resources and opportunities. Trust in governance ensures that these systems are transparent, equitable, and accountable. When leaders prioritize trust, they create a foundation for economic equity, social justice, and collective prosperity.

Building leadership rooted in trust also requires us to invest in the future. Empowering the next generation of leaders is not optional—it is essential. By mentoring young people, fostering a culture of accountability, and celebrating diverse perspectives, we ensure that the values of trust, equity, and service are carried forward. Programs that support youth leadership and community engagement are vital for cultivating a new generation of leaders who understand that trust is both a responsibility and a privilege.

As we reflect on the themes of this chapter, it is clear that leadership rooted in trust is not just an ideal—it is a necessity. It is the foundation for creating systems that work for everyone, the catalyst for building resilient communities, and the anchor that ensures governance serves the collective good. Trust transforms leadership from a position of power into an act of service, reminding us that true progress is only possible when we prioritize the well-being of others over personal gain.

Leadership rooted in trust challenges us to re-imagine what is possible. It asks us to move beyond individual ambition and embrace a vision of collective progress. It calls on us to listen, to collaborate, and to act with integrity and purpose. Most importantly, it reminds us that leadership is not about titles or positions—it is about the courage to serve, the wisdom to listen, and the commitment to build a better future.

The work of building leadership rooted in trust is ongoing. It begins with each of us—with the choices we make, the relationships we nurture, and the systems we create. By prioritizing trust, fostering collaboration, and empowering future generations, we can create a world where leadership is not a privilege, but a shared responsibility. Together, we can ensure that leadership reflects the values of love, resilience, and equity, creating a future where trust is not only a foundation but a guiding principle.

Let us step into this work with clarity and purpose, knowing that every act of trust strengthens the bonds that hold our communities together. Let us build leadership that inspires, governance that empowers, and systems that reflect the best of who we are. Trust is the bridge to a brighter future, and it begins with the choices we make today. Together, let us lead with trust and create a legacy that endures.

REFLECTION QUESTIONS

What qualities do you believe define trustworthy leadership?

How can grassroots movements inspire trust and lead to meaningful change?

In what ways can governance prioritize economic equity and justice?

Action Steps

Identify a local grassroots movement or organization and find ways to support their efforts.

Advocate for equitable resource allocation in your community by attending town halls or engaging with local leaders.

Mentor or empower a young leader in your community, sharing lessons on accountability and trust.

Notes

Chapter 11:

Trust & Justice

"Injustice anywhere is a threat to justice everywhere."

—Dr. Martin Luther King Jr.

Justice as the Foundation of Trust

Justice is the cornerstone of a fair and equitable society. It embodies the promise that every individual will be treated with dignity, fairness, and respect under the law. However, for many African Americans and marginalized communities, this promise remains unfulfilled. Instead, the justice system often serves as a source of harm and inequity, fostering mistrust and alienation rather than protection and empowerment.

This chapter explores the interplay between justice and trust, examining flaws in policing, sentencing disparities, and systemic issues within the justice system. It highlights pathways for reform, such as restorative justice practices, reentry programs, and advocacy-driven change, while grounding the conversation in real-life experiences of community engagement and systemic inequity. When truly rooted in fairness and accountability, justice has the power to heal communities and restore trust. But to make this vision a reality, it requires collective action, personal responsibility, and the courage to challenge entrenched systems.

The Cycle of Mistrust in Justice Systems
For decades, Black communities have borne the brunt of systemic inequities in the justice system. Over-policing, racial profiling, and excessive use of force have left lasting scars. Beyond policing, racial disparities in sentencing and incarceration further exacerbate mistrust, creating cycles of trauma and harm that are difficult to break. A particularly glaring issue is the ability of officers with troubling records to continue serving in law enforcement, moving from one jurisdiction to another without meaningful accountability. The story of David Wilborn, a former Lithonia police officer, illustrates this systemic loophole. Wilborn, previously employed by the Atlanta Police Department (APD), resigned in 2007 amid allegations of sexual misconduct. He was accused of visiting a lingerie shop while on duty, engaging in inappropriate behavior with an employee, and subsequently resigned before the investigation concluded. His Peace Officer Standards and Training (POST) certification was suspended from 2008 until 2010, followed by a 24-month probation. Despite this history, Wilborn was hired by the Lithonia Police Department in 2017. In 2019, while on duty, he raped a woman at gunpoint during a traffic stop in Lithonia Park. He was later convicted and sentenced to life in prison, serving 25 years without parole (11AliveNews).

This pattern—officers resigning amid allegations and finding new employment elsewhere—underscores a critical flaw in the system. Without federal oversight or a national accountability mechanism, there is little to prevent officers with problematic histories from continuing to serve. Timothy Loehmann, the officer who fatally shot 12-year-old Tamir Rice in Cleveland, Ohio, offers another example. Loehmann had been removed from the Independence Police Department after being deemed unfit for duty due to a "dangerous loss of composure" during firearms training. Despite this, he was hired by the Cleveland Police Department, where he killed Tamir Rice in 2014. After his dismissal from Cleveland in 2017 for providing false information on his application, Loehmann was hired by the Tioga Borough Police Department in Pennsylvania in 2022. However, he resigned days later amid public outcry (The Associated Press).

These examples reflect deep systemic failures in policing accountability. Without robust policies to prevent officers with histories of misconduct from remaining in law enforcement, communities are left vulnerable to harm, and trust in the justice system continues to erode. Addressing these systemic flaws requires a concerted effort from all levels of society, with both local and national actions complementing each other in a unified push for change.

Policing Reform: Closing Systemic Loopholes:

Policing reform is a critical starting point for addressing the erosion of trust in justice systems. Reform must focus on accountability, transparency, and community-centered approaches to law enforcement. However, the pursuit of reform must not rest solely on external systems or leaders—it must also involve personal accountability from individuals who are part of these systems. Those of us who live within these communities must engage in the processes that shape our justice systems to ensure fairness at every level.

Federal Oversight and National Accountability Standards:
Establishing a federal database to track officers with histories of misconduct is essential. This system would prevent officers with troubling records from transferring to other departments undetected, creating transparency and prioritizing the hiring of officers who meet ethical and professional standards.

Community-Based Policing:
Emphasizing relationship-building between officers and the communities they serve fosters trust and mutual respect. Regular interactions and community engagement encourage deescalation and nonviolent conflict resolution, showing that real reform starts not just in policies but also in the everyday interactions that foster community solidarity and connection.

Reallocating Resources to Mental Health Services:
Redirecting resources to mental health programs and deploying crisis intervention teams can reduce unnecessary police involvement and improve outcomes for individuals in distress. This initiative is a part of a larger cultural shift toward community-based safety—a shift that requires active participation from community members.

Mandatory Misconduct Insurance for Officers:
Requiring officers to carry misconduct insurance, similar to malpractice insurance for doctors, ensures financial accountability for civil rights violations. This market-based approach incentive ethical behavior while protecting taxpayers from bearing the cost of misconduct settlements.

Sentencing Reform: Addressing Racial Disparities:
Sentencing disparities remain one of the most glaring examples of systemic inequity in the justice system. Black individuals often receive harsher penalties than their white counterparts for similar offenses, perpetuating cycles of incarceration and economic disenfranchisement. Sentencing reform is a necessary step toward a more equitable justice system.

Eliminating Mandatory Minimum Sentences:
Mandatory minimum sentencing laws disproportionately impact marginalized communities, leaving judges with little discretion to consider individual circumstances. Eliminating these laws would allow for fairer and more proportional sentencing.

Expanding Alternatives to Incarceration:
Programs such as drug courts, restorative justice initiatives, and community service offer alternatives to incarceration that prioritize

rehabilitation over punishment, reducing recidivism and addressing the root causes of criminal behavior.

Restorative Justice Practices: Repairing Harm and Building Trust

Restorative justice shifts the focus from punishment to healing. By addressing harm through dialogue, accountability, and community involvement, restorative justice practices create opportunities for reconciliation and trust-building.

Community-Led Restorative Justice Programs:
Providing safe spaces for victims, offenders, and community members to engage in meaningful dialogue and accountability processes emphasizes making amends and repairing relationships. These programs offer a direct avenue for community healing, ensuring that the people most affected by injustice have the opportunity to engage in processes that promote mutual understanding.

Addressing Historical Harms:
For communities historically harmed by systemic racism and violence, restorative justice offers a way to acknowledge and address these injustices. Truth-telling and reconciliation are essential for rebuilding trust and fostering collective healing.

Reentry Programs: Supporting Second Chances:
Reentry programs are critical for supporting formerly incarcerated individuals as they transition back into society. Without adequate support, many face significant barriers to employment, housing, and education, increasing the likelihood of recidivism.

Job Training and Employment Opportunities:
Providing access to job training, apprenticeships, and employment resources helps formerly incarcerated individuals build stable lives and reduces the risk of re-offending.

Removing Barriers to Housing and Education:
Reforming policies that restrict access to housing and education for formerly incarcerated individuals is essential for successful reintegra-

tion and breaking cycles of poverty and exclusion.

The Role of Advocacy and Community Engagement

My experience serving on a citizens' committee to select a police chief for Lithonia, Georgia highlights the importance of direct community involvement in shaping justice systems. Being part of this committee provided a firsthand look at the critical differences between community-based policing—focused on relationship-building and accountability—and policy-driven policing, which often lacks a human connection to the community it serves. This experience emphasized the need for police leadership that fosters trust through engagement with the community while addressing systemic issues.

Serving on this committee also exposed troubling systemic loopholes, such as the ability of officers with problematic records to move from one department to another without accountability. These revelations underscored the need for reforms that not only promote fairness and equity but also ensure that community voices are integral in shaping policies and leadership decisions.

Advocacy is not a passive endeavor—it demands active participation, education, and a deep commitment to justice. Communities must hold leaders accountable, demand transparency in their systems, and push for reforms that align with their values. By engaging directly in processes like these, communities can build trust in justice systems and lay the foundation for meaningful, sustainable change.

Conclusion: Trust as the Foundation of Justice

Justice is more than the enforcement of laws—it is the embodiment of fairness, equity, and the collective values of a community. It is a principle that, when upheld, nurtures trust, and when violated, erodes the very fabric of society. For communities of color, the pursuit of justice is an ongoing battle, one that requires vigilance, courage, and collective action. It is not just about reforming systems; it is about re-imagining them in ways that serve and uplift everyone equally.

The stories shared in this chapter—from systemic loopholes that allow officers with troubling records to remain in the system to the challenges of building accountability in law enforcement—illustrate the complexities of achieving justice. These examples also underscore the power of advocacy, community engagement, and restorative practices in driving meaningful change. Justice is not just a matter of law enforcement; it is a shared responsibility that involves every individual, every community, and every leader working together toward a common goal.

Rebuilding trust in justice systems begins with intentionality. It requires transparent policies, equitable practices, and leaders who are willing to listen and act on behalf of the people they serve. It also requires communities to step into their power—to hold leaders accountable, demand better policies, and build systems that reflect their values.

As we reflect on the themes of this chapter, let us remember that justice is not a static ideal but a living, breathing process. It evolves as we evolve, and it demands constant effort to ensure it remains fair and inclusive. Trusting the eyes behind you means believing in the power of collective action and the potential for systems to change. It means stepping forward with courage and commitment, knowing that every act of advocacy, every push for reform, and every effort to build trust contributes to a more just and equitable society. Justice, when rooted in trust, becomes a force for transformation. It empowers communities, strengthens relationships, and lays the foundation for a brighter, more equitable future. Let this chapter serve as a call to action for all of us to engage in the work of justice—not as spectators, but as active participants in shaping a world where trust and equity prevail.

"To further explore how we can engage locally in creating meaningful police reform, see the following addendum, which offers actionable insights and strategies for leveraging local governance."

REFLECTION QUESTIONS

How has your experience with justice systems shaped your understanding of fairness and trust?

What steps can you take to advocate for more equitable policies in your community?

In what ways can restorative justice practices be integrated into your community?

How can you support reentry programs or individuals transitioning back into society after incarceration?

What role does advocacy play in creating systemic change?

Action Steps

Engage with Local Governance: Attend town hall meetings, join citizens' advisory committees, or participate in local government initiatives that influence justice systems.

Support Restorative Justice Programs: Advocate for or volunteer with organizations that promote restorative justice practices in your area.

Educate Yourself and Others: Learn about systemic inequities in policing and sentencing, and share this knowledge within your community to build awareness.

Advocate for Reentry Support: Work with organizations that provide housing, education, and job training for formerly incarcerated individuals.

Demand Policy Changes: Write to your representatives to support legislation that promotes accountability in law enforcement and equitable sentencing practices.

Notes

Chapter 12

Trust
&
Shared Leadership

"If you want to go fast, go alone. If you want to go far, go together."

— African Proverb

Building strong, thriving communities requires unity, but unity does not always mean uniformity. In fact, the diversity of experiences, perspectives, and ideas within a community can be both a strength and a challenge. Disagreements and competing visions often hinder progress, creating divisions that weaken trust and delay meaningful action. Too often, we find ourselves in situations where everyone wants to lead, but few are willing to collaborate. Trust is the key to overcoming these challenges. It enables us to work together, even when we don't always agree, and to share a common purpose despite our differences. Trust fosters the humility to step back when necessary, recognizing that leadership is not about control, but about service to a shared goal.

This chapter explores how trust is the foundation of shared leadership. It challenges the conventional view that leadership is solely about power, instead presenting it as a collaborative effort rooted in shared responsibility. By embracing this model, we can create communities where every voice is valued, where disagreements become opportunities for growth, and where trust forms the foundation of unity.

The Power of Shared Purpose and Trust

At the core of every successful community, movement, or organization is a shared purpose—a unifying goal that brings people together. A shared purpose provides meaning to our work, guides our efforts, and inspires us to move beyond personal ambitions in pursuit of the greater good. However, shared purpose does not require uniformity in thought or action. The diversity of ideas and experiences within a group often strengthens the collective effort by introducing new solutions and perspectives. Trust plays a central role in this process. When trust exists, people are able to approach disagreements with humility, recognizing that differing viewpoints are opportunities for growth rather than threats. Trust also fosters accountability, ensuring that everyone remains focused on the collective purpose, rather than personal agendas.

The African American leadership tradition, with its roots in communal bonds, exemplifies the importance of shared purpose. For example, organizations like 100 Black Men of America work to bring together people from different walks of life with a singular focus on the upliftment of African American youth. Their approach highlights how shared leadership and a unified purpose can address collective goals. These organizations succeed because they recognize that leadership is not about individual control, but about the collective effort of many people working toward a common good.

In communities rooted in African and African American traditions, trust is the foundation of collective action. As Dr. Patricia Hill Collins discusses in Black Feminist Thought, African American leadership has often been about service to the community, where leaders empower others to act, and not about the centralization of power. This tradition teaches us that when trust exists, differences are seen as opportunities for learning, not obstacles to overcome. It's through these diverse perspectives that we truly build a unified, strong community.

Leaders like Stokely Carmichael (Kwame Ture) and Kwame Nkrumah exemplify the power of shared leadership in the context of African liberation and social justice. Carmichael's call for Black Power emphasized the need for a unified, collective effort in which leadership was not the domain of a single individual, but shared by the people. His approach underscored the importance of grassroots involvement and community empowerment, trusting that the collective strength of the people would lead to transformative change. Similarly, Kwame Nkrumah, the first President of Ghana, promoted Pan-Africanism and collective self-reliance. His vision for Africa as a united continent reflected his belief that true progress would come from shared leadership across national borders, rooted in the trust of the people to work together for a common purpose.

Clarity Over Agreement: Diverse Approaches to Leadership

The concept that "clarity is better than agreement" resonates deeply when we think about shared leadership. In many organizations, movements, and governments, unity doesn't always mean everyone agreeing on every detail or taking the same approach. What is essential is the clarity of the collective vision—the purpose that drives everyone forward. We see this in the work of social movements and political organizations, where diverse leadership approaches can coexist when there is clarity in the shared mission.

This idea is mirrored in the way the Federal Government operates. The State Department and the Department of Defense (DOD) have different functions and approaches, yet they are both essential to the success of national policy. The State Department is responsible for diplomacy—negotiating treaties, building relationships, and advocating for peaceful solutions, while the Department of Defense manages national security, military operations, and defense strategy. Both departments serve shared national interests but often employ different strategies, yet both are vital to the success of the government's goals. They work in tandem, despite having differing approaches, because there is clarity of purpose and shared vision—to ensure the nation's well-being and international standing.

The Civil Rights Movement saw leaders like Martin Luther King Jr. and Malcolm X embodying the roles of diplomats and warriors, each playing a complementary role in the larger struggle for justice and equality. King, the diplomat, engaged in non-violent resistance, sitting at tables with political leaders and pushing for systemic change through legal reforms. Malcolm X, as part of the Nation of Islam, was the warrior—demanding respect, autonomy, and equality through direct action, including self-defense. Despite their differences in approach, both were working toward the same goal—justice and equality for African Americans.

The Diplomat-Warrior dynamic embodied by King and Malcolm X illustrates how seemingly opposing methods can actually complement each other when there is a shared commitment to a larger mission. But the struggle didn't end with these two figures—Stokely Carmichael (Kwame Ture) and Kwame Nkrumah also played pivotal roles, providing further depth to the warrior approach and broadening the international scope of the fight for justice.

Stokely Carmichael (Kwame Ture) and Kwame Nkrumah: Broadening the Vision

Stokely Carmichael, later known as Kwame Ture, was a leading figure in the Black Power Movement, and his philosophy extended beyond just advocating for African American rights. Carmichael emphasized the necessity of self-determination, Black autonomy, and revolutionary change. His powerful call for Black Power was not a rejection of the work of King but a reinforcement of the idea that diverse leadership styles could unite to advance the cause of Black liberation. Carmichael's call for Black Power was revolutionary because it didn't just advocate for social justice within the confines of the United States but challenged the very global structures that oppressed people of African descent.

His efforts paralleled Malcolm X's in some ways, as both leaders advocated for self-defense and revolutionary action in the face of systemic violence. However, Carmichael's push for Pan-African unity and global liberation took the struggle from local to international. The urgency of his philosophy drove many in the movement to see their struggles as interconnected with those of Africans around the world. Kwame Ture's emphasis on the need for a worldwide Black revolution and his collaboration with African leaders like Kwame Nkrumah exemplified the expansion of the warrior's reach—his work transcended national borders and made the call for justice truly global.

Kwame Nkrumah, the first president of Ghana, also embodied the warrior spirit in his Pan-Africanist vision. Nkrumah's leadership was grounded in the belief that African unity was critical for the success of the entire continent, and he believed that the African diaspora, including African Americans, had a crucial role in this struggle. Like Carmichael, Nkrumah was not simply fighting for civil rights within one nation, but for a unified African continent and the self-determination of all African peoples, both at home and abroad. His philosophy of "Consciencism", which emphasized the importance of African identity and economic independence, was a powerful call to action for people of African descent to take ownership of their future.

Nkrumah's global view complemented the work being done in the United States by King, Malcolm X, and Carmichael. He created opportunities for cross-continental dialogue, furthering the Pan-African movement that sought not only independence for African nations but also liberation for Africans everywhere. In this way, the warrior model of leadership—embodied by Carmichael and Nkrumah—pushed the vision for Black liberation to a global scale, calling for solidarity among oppressed peoples and linking the struggles of African Americans to those of Africans and Black people worldwide.

Diplomats and Warriors Together

Just as the State Department and Department of Defense work in parallel to ensure national security, the diplomats and warriors in the Civil Rights Movement worked hand-in-hand to create the necessary momentum for change. While King sought negotiation and peaceful protests, Malcolm X, Stokely Carmichael, and others like the Black Panther Party created direct pressure, demanding equality and justice from the government. The interdependency between these different leadership approaches created a dynamic force that made it impossible for the government to ignore the growing demand for civil rights.

Both King's non-violent protests and the revolutionary stances of Malcolm X, Stokely Carmichael, and the Black Panther Party created a groundswell of energy that moved the Civil Rights Movement forward. Together, they formed a complementary force that pressured the government to pass landmark civil rights legislation such as the Civil Rights Act of 1964 and the Voting Rights Act of 1965. This dynamic teaches us that leadership, no matter the approach, must ultimately serve the collective purpose—and when different forms of leadership work together, they can achieve monumental change.

Building Consensus Through Trust

One of the most important skills in any community or organization is consensus-building. Finding common ground, navigating disagreements, and aligning around a shared vision are essential for collective progress. But consensus-building is not always as simple as it sounds. It requires more than just agreement—it requires the ability to understand different perspectives, manage differences in a way that fosters unity, and move forward with a collective sense of purpose. In communities grounded in trust, consensus-building is not about winning arguments or overpowering others—it's about listening, understanding, and seeking solutions that serve the collective good.

The process of consensus-building is dynamic and requires a nuanced approach. It involves people from diverse backgrounds and perspectives coming together to discuss their needs, concerns, and hopes for the future. In these discussions, people must feel heard, respected, and included in the decision-making process. The ability to listen actively, without judgment, is one of the most critical components of successful consensus-building. When individuals feel heard and understood, the trust between them grows, allowing for greater collaboration and the creation of solutions that benefit the whole. In many communities, particularly those facing systemic oppression or historical divisions, trust can be difficult to establish. It requires a commitment to vulnerability, an openness to not just listen but also to understand and empathize with the experiences of others. Trust cannot be demanded—it must be earned through consistent, transparent actions and through demonstrating a commitment to the well-being of the entire group. This is why communities grounded in trust are more effective at navigating difficult conversations and forging deeper connections. Trust creates a safe space where people feel confident enough to share their thoughts, express their concerns, and challenge ideas without fear of judgment or exclusion.

To achieve true consensus, communities must create environments where everyone has the opportunity to engage in open dialogue. Dialogue is the foundation of consensus-building, but it is not always easy. It requires active listening, empathy, and respect for every voice, regardless of social status, experience, or perspective. In a community where trust is present, constructive dialogue can thrive. It allows the group to navigate disagreements without becoming entrenched in conflict. When people trust one another, they are more likely to accept differing views, seek common ground, and work collaboratively toward solutions. As John Lewis once said, "We may not have the same ideas, but we are all here to build a future together." This philosophy of unity amid difference is central to effective consensus-building.

The Role of Humility and Service in Consensus Building

A significant barrier to consensus is ego—the tendency to prioritize personal ideas, desires, or ambitions over the collective purpose. When individuals place their own goals above those of the community, it creates division, mistrust, and stagnation. In the process of consensus-building, humility plays a pivotal role. It is the willingness to set aside personal ambitions for the sake of the greater good, a quality that enables true collaboration and effective decision-making. Humility allows us to acknowledge that leadership is not about control, status, or personal validation, but rather about service to the community. When leaders practice humility, they create an environment where individuals can openly disagree without fear of feeling attacked or dismissed.

In communities grounded in trust, disagreements are seen as opportunities to deepen understanding, rather than sources of conflict. In fact, disagreement in a trusting community can serve as a catalyst for growth—a chance to refine ideas, align goals, and strengthen collective resolve. When people are humble and approach disagreements with an open heart and mind, they foster unity despite differing perspectives. This approach doesn't mean that every decision will be made easily, or that everyone will always agree. But it does create a shared commitment to the common good, allowing individuals to see past personal interests and focus on serving the collective purpose. This mindset of service lies at the heart of what makes a community strong. True leadership, whether in social movements, organizations, or local communities, is about serving the collective. It involves facilitating collaboration, amplifying the voices of others, and ensuring that the shared vision remains at the center of every decision. Leaders who adopt this approach do not seek to control or dominate the group, but to guide, support, and enable the community to move forward. They model humility, transparency, and collaboration, thereby creating a culture where everyone feels valued and empowered to contribute. When leaders exemplify this mindset, they inspire others to follow suit, creating a ripple effect that strengthens the entire community.

True leaders do not hold the weight of responsibility alone—they encourage and empower others to lead. This distributed model of leadership ensures that no single person bears the burden of decision-making. Instead, everyone has a voice and an opportunity to step into leadership roles when the situation calls for it. Leadership is not about directing or controlling others; it is about showing what is possible and inviting others to share in that vision. Leaders who demonstrate trust, accountability, and collaboration create a culture of shared responsibility, where collective success becomes not just the leader's goal, but the community's collective achievement.

Fellowing and Overcoming Leadership Competition

While much attention is often given to leadership, following is equally crucial to the success of any community or movement. A strong community requires not only effective leaders but also engaged followers who trust in the vision and are willing to contribute their time, energy, and skills to its realization. Following, however, is not passive. It is active, deeply involved, and integral to the community's success. Following begins with trust—followers must trust that their leaders have the best interests of the community at heart and are working toward a shared purpose. This trust is built through transparency, accountability, and consistent actions that demonstrate the leader's commitment to the collective good.

Active participation from followers is what transforms a group of people into a cohesive force. Followers contribute their talents, ideas, and energy to the collective effort, ensuring that the vision becomes a reality. When followers are actively engaged, they not only strengthen the leadership but also take ownership of the collective mission. This sense of shared ownership is what creates strong, sustainable communities where everyone feels invested in the outcome. Trust is the foundation that allows following to be active, rather than passive, because it provides the assurance that the effort will serve the collective good.

A common challenge in many communities is the tendency toward leadership competition. This often arises when individuals vie for control or recognition, creating unnecessary conflict and stagnation. When everyone seeks to lead but no one is willing to collaborate, the collective effort breaks down, and trust erodes. To overcome this dynamic, communities must embrace the idea that every role is valuable. Leadership is not about titles or personal recognition—it is about taking responsibility for the collective good. Every member of the community, regardless of their official title or role, has something valuable to contribute.

Trust is essential in this process, as it allows individuals to step into the roles that best serve the community, without fear that their contributions will be overlooked or undervalued. When trust is present, individuals are more likely to embrace their roles and work collaboratively toward the common purpose. They know that their voices will be heard, and that their efforts will be appreciated. This atmosphere of collaboration over competition helps to minimize the fractures caused by ego and self-interest, allowing the community to move forward with a shared vision of success.

Conclusion

Building strong, resilient communities requires more than just a shared space—it requires shared purpose, humility, and trust. These are the cornerstones upon which collective progress is built. We may not always agree on every approach, nor should we expect to, but the power of trust enables us to work together despite our differences. It allows us to align around a common vision and contribute to its success, knowing that the whole is greater than the sum of its parts. In communities grounded in trust, we recognize that leadership is not about control, and following is not about passivity. Rather, both are about service to the collective good—putting the needs of the community before personal gain and lifting each other up as we all strive toward a shared goal.

However, trust and collaboration are not just ideals—they are practices that require tangible action. One of the most important ways we can engage with the principle of shared leadership is through local, community-driven efforts. For example, police reform begins at the local level, where leaders and citizens alike can work together to create a safer and more just community for all. By participating in local governance and advocating for meaningful policy change, we embody the principles of collective action, trust, and accountability. Take the first step today: research your city's charter, understand your local governance structures, and start advocating for change. Whether it's engaging in local elections, pushing for more transparent police practices, or holding elected officials accountable, your involvement is critical. Together, we can move beyond personal ambitions and build a future rooted in trust and fairness.

REFLECTION QUESTIONS

What role does trust play in your approach to leadership and collaboration?

Reflect on specific instances where trust was a factor in either the success or challenge of a project or relationship.

In what ways can you encourage open dialogue within your community or organization?

Consider practical strategies that create safe spaces for diverse perspectives to be shared and heard.

How can you balance leadership and following within your collective efforts?

Reflect on your role as both a leader and a follower, and how these roles contribute to collective progress.

How do you approach disagreements in ways that strengthen, rather than weaken, trust?

Think of situations where you disagreed and how you responded to ensure respect and unity.

What actions can you take to ensure that all voices are heard and valued in your community?

Consider steps to actively include underrepresented voices or perspectives and build a culture of inclusion.

Action Steps

Host a Collaborative Visioning Session: Create spaces where community members can share their ideas, concerns, and aspirations, and work toward a collective vision. Ensure the session emphasizes the value of diversity and shared responsibility.

Develop Leadership Training Programs: Focus on cultivating trust, humility, and collaboration in future leaders, equipping them with the skills to foster inclusive environments and lead through service.

Celebrate the Diversity of Leadership Roles: Acknowledge and honor the contributions of all members, not just those in formal leadership positions, recognizing the strength in diverse approaches to leadership.

Encourage Constructive Feedback and Reflection: Build systems for open and respectful feedback between leaders and community members, creating opportunities for both to learn from each other and grow.

Model Collaborative Leadership: Demonstrate the values of shared responsibility, transparency, and trust in your actions and decisions, setting an example for others to follow and creating a ripple effect of collaborative action.

Notes

Chapter 13:

Trust & Legacy

"To each generation is entrusted the future of the race."

— Anna Julia Cooper

Building a Legacy of Trust

A legacy is more than what you leave behind—it is the foundation you create for those who follow. Legacy is about planting seeds for a future you may never see, trusting that the work you do today will bear fruit for generations to come. For communities of African descent, legacy is deeply tied to resilience, cultural preservation, and the unbroken chain of wisdom passed down through the ages. Legacy is not just about wealth or achievements. It is about values, practices, and relationships rooted in trust. Whether your spiritual foundation lies in African traditions, Christianity, or another path, the principles of trust, love, and service are universal. They are the threads that weave a strong legacy, ensuring that future generations inherit not just material success but also the tools to thrive spiritually, emotionally, and culturally.

The concept of legacy is not static; it evolves with each generation. Dr. Maulana Karenga, the creator of Kwanzaa, emphasizes the importance of kujichagulia, (self-determination) in building a legacy: "To leave a legacy is to be actively engaged in the making of a future that reflects our highest values and aspirations." This requires a deliberate commitment to shaping the world we want to pass on.

The Role of Spiritual Trust in Legacy

Spiritual trust is the invisible thread that connects the past, present, and future, weaving together resilience, wisdom, and divine purpose. It anchors communities in a sense of belonging and continuity, offering the assurance that the sacrifices of those who came before us were not in vain and that the work we do today will endure. This trust is not abstract; it finds expression in practices that honor ancestors as vital participants in shaping legacy.

In African spiritual traditions, the role of ancestors extends beyond remembrance, they are considered active participants in the lives of the living. Through libation ceremonies, oral storytelling, and rituals, African communities honor their ancestors as guardians of values, protectors of traditions, and sources of spiritual guidance. These practices ensure that legacy is a living, evolving force. Dr. Wade Nobles, a leading scholar in African-centered psychology, describes the concept of **ntu** in his work. This Bantu term reflects the interconnectedness of all life and emphasizes the spiritual dimension of legacy. "We stand on the shoulders of giants," Nobles writes, "not just to see further, but to carry their vision into the future." This spiritual trust transforms individual lives into a continuum of collective purpose.

This philosophy of interconnectedness also finds resonance in the African American spiritual tradition, particularly through the enduring strength of the Black Church. From its inception, the Black Church has served as both a sanctuary and a center of community resilience. Leaders like Rev. Dr. Martin Luther King Jr. emphasized the importance of faith as a catalyst for social change, connecting spiritual trust to the broader mission of justice and equality. The Black Church's mission of collective resilience mirrors the Christian principle of stewardship, which emphasizes responsibility and care as acts of trust.

The Christian principle of stewardship highlights the importance of trust and responsibility in building a legacy. Theologian Howard Thurman framed stewardship as a spiritual mandate, urging individuals to care for their resources, relationships, and communities as sacred trusts. "We do not own the world," Thurman wrote. "We are caretakers, and our legacy is in the care we extend." Stewardship challenges individuals to think beyond personal gain, emphasizing the collective good and the well-being of future generations. This principle is reflected in the work of freedom fighters like Sojourner Truth and Harriet Tubman, who saw their missions as divinely ordained acts of trust and service. Their legacies endure because they were rooted in faith and guided by a vision of liberation that extended beyond their lifetimes.

Legacy, however, is not static. It evolves with each generation, requiring spiritual trust that future generations will carry forward the values and lessons of the past while adapting them to meet new challenges. In the Yoruba tradition, the concept of ase speaks to the divine authority within each individual to create and shape their destiny. This belief fosters a sense of responsibility and trust in one's ability to contribute to the collective legacy.

The Akan concept of Sankofa—symbolized by a bird looking backward, while flying forward—offers a complementary perspective, emphasizing the power to shape destiny, while drawing wisdom from the past. Trusting in spiritual principles allows communities to navigate the uncertainties of the present with the assurance that their legacy is both resilient and adaptable.

Building a Legacy Rooted in Trust

Building a legacy is a deliberate and ongoing process, one that requires intentional actions, meaningful relationships, and a commitment to values that transcend individual lives. Trust is the cornerstone of this process, shaping how individuals and communities envision and construct the futures they hope to leave behind.

This trust is first cultivated through the preservation and sharing of cultural knowledge—a vital act of resistance against erasure and a celebration of identity. By safeguarding traditions, languages, and practices, communities ensure that their identities endure, even in the face of change. Families often play a pivotal role, passing down stories, recipes, songs, and rituals that encapsulate the essence of their heritage.

Dr. Molefi Kete Asante, a pioneer of Afrocentric thought, argues in Afrocentricity: The Theory of Social Change that reclaiming and teaching African history and culture is both an act of empowerment and a way to remain grounded in truth. "A legacy rooted in trust," Asante writes, "is one that keeps its people grounded in their truth, even as they navigate a changing world." The Gullah-Geechee Cultural Heritage Corridor exemplifies this principle, preserving unique language, crafts, and traditions to inspire future generations with a legacy of cultural resilience.

Preserving cultural knowledge, however, is only one facet of building a meaningful legacy. True legacy is incomplete without investment in the next generation. This investment manifests in many forms—mentorship, education, advocacy, and leadership development—all of which equip young people to carry the torch and shape their futures. Educator Carter G. Woodson, known as the Father of Black History, championed the transformative power of education in shaping legacy. In The Mis-Education of the Negro, Woodson wrote, "The real servant of the people is the one who makes himself unnecessary. Teach children so well that they no longer need you but carry forward the mission with integrity."

Programs like My Brother's Keeper and organizations such as the Black Youth Project 100 (BYP100) exemplify this investment. By providing resources, mentorship, and platforms for advocacy, these initiatives amplify the voices of young leaders, enabling them to honor their roots while forging their own paths. This act of trust ensures that each generation is better positioned to contribute to and expand the legacy of their communities.

The Eternal Nature of Legacy

Legacy is timeless. It is the invisible thread that ties generations together, weaving a tapestry of values, sacrifices, and aspirations that transcend the limitations of time and space. The trust you build today shapes the future, just as the sacrifices of your ancestors shaped your present. Spiritual trust ensures that your legacy is rooted in something eternal—values like love, resilience, and connection that endure across generations, providing a foundation upon which the future can flourish.

This eternal quality of legacy finds its most profound expression in acts of collective transformation. Consider the enduring influence of social justice leaders like Ella Baker and Fannie Lou Hamer. Their unwavering commitment to trust, community-building, and justice forged pathways for change that extend far beyond their lifetimes. Baker's grassroots organizing philosophy—"strong people don't need strong leaders"—emphasized empowering communities to become self-sufficient and resilient. Hamer's courage, born from a deeply rooted trust in her faith and her people, inspired countless others to join the fight for civil rights. Their legacies remind us that true impact is measured not in accolades but in the strength and unity they instill in others.

The legacy of such leaders is not confined to history books; it lives on in the movements they inspired. Organizations advocating for equity and justice today are the direct beneficiaries of their trust in collective progress. They teach us that legacy is not about self-serving ambition but about creating an ecosystem of support, where each contribution adds to the strength and resilience of the whole. Every protest, every policy change, every community program becomes a seed planted in the soil of trust—a seed that will bear fruit for generations to come.

As you reflect on your own legacy, it is vital to ask: What seeds am I planting today? How will they grow? Are my actions rooted in the kind of trust that ensures longevity and sustainability? These questions guide us toward purposeful action, helping us understand that legacy-building is not a passive endeavor but a deliberate act of creation. Legacy is not simply about leaving something behind; it is about ensuring that what you leave behind has the power to sustain, nurture, and inspire those who come after you.

A legacy rooted in trust is one that endures, connecting the wisdom of the past with the possibilities of the future. Such a legacy ensures that each generation inherits not just material wealth but also the spiritual, emotional, and cultural tools to thrive. Dr. John Henrik Clarke captured the essence of this idea when he said, "A people's relationship to their heritage is the same as the relationship of a child to its mother." Heritage is not just a collection of stories or artifacts—it is a source of nourishment, strength, and identity. Nurturing this relationship ensures that future generations inherit not only the material benefits of our labor but also the spiritual and cultural wealth that sustains them.

Trusting the eyes behind you is not just about looking back with gratitude; it is about moving forward with conviction. It means believing that the work you do today—however small or unseen—will ripple out into eternity, leaving a world that is better, brighter, and more connected for those who follow. Legacy is built on this trust: the trust that every action, every sacrifice, and every intention will serve as a stepping stone for someone else's journey.

Building a legacy rooted in trust also demands humility and foresight. It requires us to recognize that we are part of a continuum, one chapter in a much larger story. When we align our actions with values that honor this continuum, we contribute to something far greater than ourselves. By investing in community, preserving cultural wisdom, and living out the principles of service and love, we create a legacy that cannot be erased.

This is the work that transcends time and space. It is the work of honoring our ancestors, uplifting our communities, and creating a foundation for future generations to thrive. A legacy rooted in trust is one that endures, not because it is perfect, but because it is built with intention, resilience, and an unwavering belief in the potential of those who will carry it forward. As we plant the seeds of our legacy, let us do so with the knowledge that we are shaping the future, ensuring that our impact is as eternal as the trust we cultivate today.

Conclusion: A Legacy Built on Trust

Legacy is not a destination; it is an ongoing journey, a sacred responsibility carried by each generation to honor the past and shape the future. A legacy rooted in trust bridges time, connecting the wisdom and sacrifices of our ancestors with the aspirations and possibilities of those yet to come. It is built not on material wealth alone but on enduring values—love, resilience, and service—that nurture and sustain communities.

To build such a legacy requires intentional action and unwavering commitment. It means preserving cultural knowledge, investing in future generations, and living out principles that reflect our deepest values. It is about planting seeds in soil enriched by the sacrifices of those who came before us, trusting that they will grow into a future of pride, strength, and unity.

Dr. John Henrik Clarke's words remind us of the profound connection between heritage and identity: "A people's relationship to their heritage is the same as the relationship of a child to its mother." To nurture that heritage is to ensure that future generations inherit not just stories and traditions but also the spiritual and cultural wealth needed to thrive. It is an act of trust in the unbroken chain of resilience that binds us together.

This legacy of trust is more than a reflection on the past—it is a responsibility to the future. Every small action, every act of service, and every moment of love contributes to a foundation that will uplift those who follow. A legacy built on trust does not end with us; it flows forward, carrying the power of our intentions into eternity, transforming aspirations into lasting impact.

A legacy rooted in trust is one that endures, one that echoes across time, shaping a world that reflects the best of who we are and what we aspire to be. Let us plant the seeds of that legacy today, knowing that its fruits will nourish and sustain the future.

REFLECTION QUESTIONS

What values and practices do you want to pass on to future generations?

How does your spiritual or cultural foundation inform your understanding of legacy?

What deliberate actions can you take today to ensure your legacy reflects your values and aspirations?

Action Steps

Document your family history, ensuring stories and traditions are preserved for future generations.

Mentor a young person in your community, sharing lessons of resilience and empowerment.

Support or create a program or institution that reflects your values and contributes to the well-being of others.

Notes

Chapter 14

Building the Future: The Intentionality of Legacy

"The best way to predict the future is to create it."

- Peter Drucker

The Foundation of Tomorrow

The future is not a distant destination—it is an evolving reality shaped by the decisions, actions, and commitments we make today. It is not something that arrives unbidden; it is something we build intentionally, brick by brick, through the values we uphold, the relationships we nurture, and the systems we create. At the heart of this construction lies trust: the thread that binds generations, connects communities, and serves as the foundation for lasting progress. Trust is not merely a philosophical ideal; it is the engine that drives meaningful change and the glue that holds together the vision of a better world.

Without trust, progress stalls. It is trust that fuels collaboration, sustains momentum, and makes collective action possible. It is the belief in one another and in the systems we build that allows us to envision a future of shared purpose and possibility. When trust is absent, efforts fragment, relationships deteriorate, and legacies falter. But when trust is cultivated and nurtured, it becomes a transformative force—a foundation upon which meaningful change can be realized.

Throughout this book, we have examined trust in its many dimensions: within ourselves, our families, our communities, and the broader systems and institutions that shape our lives. We have seen how trust builds resilience in times of adversity, fosters connection in the face of division, and drives accountability in the pursuit of equity and justice. Each chapter has revealed a different facet of trust, illuminating its role as both a guiding principle and a powerful tool for action. Now, as we approach the culmination of these discussions, we turn our attention to the future and to the practical steps required to bring trust to life in our daily actions and aspirations.

Building the future is not a solitary endeavor. It is not the work of one individual, one generation, or even one community—it is a shared responsibility that calls upon us all. It demands that we look beyond our immediate circumstances and personal interests, weaving together the lessons of the past, the realities of the present, and the boundless possibilities of the future. This work requires not only intention but also collaboration, as the challenges we face are too complex to be solved in isolation. Trust becomes the common ground upon which diverse perspectives can converge, enabling the collective action needed to drive meaningful progress.

The lessons of the past remind us that trust has always been a catalyst for transformation. From the grassroots movements that challenged systems of oppression to the quiet acts of care and connection that sustained families and communities through generations, trust has been the force that turned adversity into opportunity. These lessons are not relics of history; they are blueprints for the work that lies ahead. They remind us that trust is both a gift we inherit and a responsibility we must uphold—a foundation that must be continually reinforced through our actions.

As we look to the future, we must recognize that building trust is both an individual and a collective endeavor. It begins with self-trust: the confidence to align our actions with our values and to take risks in pursuit of a greater purpose. It extends outward, shaping the ways we connect with others, the systems we create, and the legacies we leave behind. It calls on us to be intentional in our efforts, resilient in the face of challenges, and unwavering in our commitment to the principles that guide us.

This chapter invites us to move from reflection to action, from vision to implementation. It challenges us to consider how trust can guide our decisions, shape our relationships, and empower us to build systems that reflect our highest ideals. It reminds us that the work of creating a better future is not about perfection; it is about persistence, collaboration, and the courage to act. Together, we can weave a narrative of progress and purpose—one rooted in trust and carried forward by the collective strength of our communities.

The foundation of tomorrow is laid today. Each action we take, each connection we nurture, and each system we shape contributes to the reality we are creating. Trust is the cornerstone of this work, the force that transforms aspirations into achievements and visions into reality. Let us move forward with clarity, purpose, and a steadfast commitment to building a future where trust is not only cultivated but celebrated as the foundation of progress and possibility.

Trust as the Foundation of Progress

Trust is not merely a value—it is an active, dynamic force that drives action and sustains momentum. It underpins relationships, fortifies institutions, and provides the stability needed for collective progress. As the glue that holds communities together, trust forms the framework for justice and equity and fuels the engines of systemic change.

Without trust, movements falter, relationships crumble, and legacies fail to endure, leaving gaps in the foundation of progress. Reflecting on Chapter 4, the spiritual dimensions of trust emerge as an essential bridge to our higher selves. Trust enables individuals to rise above fear and uncertainty, embracing clarity, purpose, and a sense of connection that transcends immediate challenges. Dr. Marimba Ani notes that trust within the spiritual realm roots individuals in their culture and history, empowering them to confront the complexities of the present. This spiritual trust, anchored in resilience and guided by inherited wisdom, becomes the cornerstone of personal growth and collective advancement. It equips us with the fortitude to embrace change while remaining deeply connected to the values that define us.

In Chapter 8, the relationship between trust and governance illuminated how accountability and equity stem from leaders who embody and inspire trust. Such leaders foster collaboration, empower communities, and create structures that ensure collective well-being. Consider leaders like Shirley Chisholm, who declared herself "unbought and unbossed," a testament to the integrity and trust she championed in her public service. Trust in leadership is not just a catalyst for progress but a vital safeguard against complacency and corruption, ensuring that systems serve the collective good. Progress, however, is rarely a straight path. It demands resilience and adaptability, qualities only made possible through trust. Progress requires the courage to face setbacks, learn from failures, and persist through adversity. Trust provides the emotional and psychological stability needed to sustain movements, inspire action, and maintain focus. For example, the Montgomery Bus Boycott demonstrated how trust in shared values and leadership sustained an extended movement that ultimately transformed systemic inequities. Trust is the silent yet powerful force that underpins social transformations, ensuring that each step forward is grounded in collective strength and unity.

Trust also drives innovation. When trust permeates a community, individuals feel safe to take risks, propose bold ideas, and challenge conventional thinking. This environment of trust becomes the breeding ground for transformative solutions that address systemic barriers and pave the way for enduring change. For example, the Freedom Schools during the Civil Rights Movement exemplified how trust and collaboration empowered communities to innovate in education and build a new generation of leaders. Trust is not static; it is a dynamic force that grows as it is nurtured and applied.

Finally, trust sustains momentum. As movements evolve and expand, trust ensures alignment between goals and actions. It prevents fragmentation, fostering solidarity among diverse groups working toward a common purpose. The shared trust among participants in the Civil Rights Movement created the cohesion necessary to achieve landmark victories like the Voting Rights Act and the Civil Rights Act. These achievements underscore the centrality of trust as a foundation for progress, proving that its presence strengthens every aspect of social change.

Trust is not merely a value—it is an active, dynamic force that drives action and sustains momentum. It underpins relationships, fortifies institutions, and provides the stability needed for collective progress. As the glue that holds communities together, trust forms the framework for justice and equity and fuels the engines of systemic change. Without trust, movements falter, relationships crumble, and legacies fail to endure, leaving gaps in the foundation of progress. Progress, however, is rarely a straight path. It demands resilience and adaptability, qualities only made possible through trust. Progress requires the courage to face setbacks, learn from failures, and persist through adversity. Trust provides the emotional and psychological stability needed to sustain movements, inspire action, and maintain focus. It is the silent yet powerful force that underpins social transformations, ensuring that each step forward is grounded in collective strength and unity.

Trust also drives innovation. Consider the role trust plays in fostering creativity and collaboration within movements for justice and equality. When trust permeates a community, individuals feel safe to take risks, propose bold ideas, and challenge conventional thinking. This environment of trust becomes the breeding ground for transformative solutions that address systemic barriers and pave the way for enduring change. Trust is not static; it is a dynamic force that grows as it is nurtured and applied.

Finally, trust sustains momentum. As movements evolve and expand, trust ensures alignment between goals and actions. It prevents fragmentation, fostering solidarity among diverse groups working toward a common purpose. For example, the trust shared among participants in the Civil Rights Movement created the cohesion necessary to achieve landmark victories like the Voting Rights Act and the Civil Rights Act. These achievements underscore the centrality of trust as a foundation for progress, proving that its presence strengthens every aspect of social change.

Passing the Torch: A Legacy of Trust

Legacy is not a static inheritance but a dynamic, evolving process that requires building, adapting, and passing the torch to those who come after us. As explored in Chapter 11, legacy encompasses far more than material wealth. It is the enduring transmission of values, relationships, and systems that reflect the collective journey of a people. At its core, building a legacy of trust involves equipping future generations with the tools to sustain and innovate, ensuring that progress remains continuous and impactful.

Preparation is at the heart of effective succession. Movements and institutions often falter not because they lack purpose, but because they lack foresight. Leadership transitions are critical junctures that require careful planning, humility, and an unwavering commitment to the greater good. Leaders must trust that the time will come to pass the torch and dedicate themselves to preparing their successors. This preparation involves mentorship, skill development, and a shared vision for the future. The absence of such intentionality risks stagnation and the erosion of progress.

Frantz Fanon's insight, "Each generation, out of relative obscurity, must discover its mission, fulfill it or betray it," underscores the urgency of intergenerational collaboration. Elders bear the responsibility of sharing their wisdom and experiences, creating a foundation of trust that empowers younger generations to take action. Simultaneously, the younger generation must approach this wisdom with respect, while contributing fresh perspectives and energy to adapt to new challenges. This delicate balance of honoring the past while innovating for the future is the essence of a thriving legacy. Trust is the unifying thread in this intergenerational exchange. Leaders must believe in the potential of their successors, and successors must honor the vision of their predecessors. This mutual trust fosters a powerful synergy, where the collective strength of the community is greater than the sum of its parts. By trusting others to lead, elders ensure continuity while allowing space for growth and evolution.

Successors, in turn, must embrace the responsibility of carrying the torch with integrity and vision.

Examples of successful transitions reveal the transformative power of trust in action. Consider the African American Church, where leadership transitions often occur within a framework of mentorship and community support. This system ensures that each new leader inherits not just a role but a legacy of trust and responsibility to the congregation. Such intentional transitions preserve the integrity of institutions while allowing them to evolve in response to changing circumstances.

The failure to prepare for succession, on the other hand, can have dire consequences. History is replete with examples of movements and organizations that lost momentum due to fragmented leadership or unprepared successors. Trust ensures that transitions are not moments of vulnerability but opportunities for renewal and growth. Leaders who approach succession with humility and foresight contribute to a legacy that is both enduring and adaptable. Trust also enables collective resilience during transitions. When communities trust in their leaders and the processes guiding succession, they remain united and focused on shared goals. This trust mitigates the uncertainties and tensions that often accompany change, ensuring that the community moves forward with strength and cohesion. Passing the torch is not a relinquishment of responsibility; it is an affirmation of faith in the enduring power of the community.
In building a legacy of trust, we are reminded that leadership is not about individual achievement but collective empowerment. Leaders who understand this cultivate trust not just in their actions but in the systems they leave behind. They recognize that the true measure of leadership is the ability to inspire trust that transcends their tenure, ensuring that progress continues to thrive long after they are gone.

Transforming Ideas into Action

Ideas are the seeds of change, but action is what brings them to life. Throughout this book, we have explored the importance of vision, leadership, and accountability in building systems of trust. Now, we turn to the practical steps required to transform these ideas into action. Trust is the connective tissue that makes this transformation possible, bridging the gap between conceptual understanding and meaningful progress.

Trust begins within. As discussed in Chapter 2, cultivating self-trust is the foundational step toward aligning actions with values and purpose. When we trust ourselves, we unlock the courage to take risks, embrace vulnerability, and learn from failure. These qualities are not just beneficial but essential for progress. Self-trust acts as the internal compass that guides decision-making, ensuring that our actions are rooted in integrity and resilience. For example, the journeys of leaders like Ella Baker demonstrate how self-trust fosters the ability to lead with authenticity, even amidst adversity. It is this internal alignment that empowers us to trust others and to take bold steps toward creating a better future.

Collaboration is the lifeblood of progress. As we explored in Chapter 10, shared leadership and collective action are vital for building strong communities. No single individual can achieve systemic change alone. By pooling resources, ideas, and talents, we create a synergistic foundation of trust that amplifies our collective impact. This shift from individual interests to shared goals requires a deliberate embrace of equity and justice. For instance, movements like the Civil Rights Movement exemplify the transformative power of collective action. Activists like Fannie Lou Hamer and John Lewis understood that collaboration was not just a strategy but a necessity. Their efforts remind us that trust is both the precondition and the outcome of working together toward a shared vision.

Accountability serves as the cornerstone of trust. Without it, even the most well-intentioned efforts risk faltering under the weight of unchecked power or misaligned priorities. Chapter 9 highlighted how systems of accountability ensure that actions align with values and that progress remains sustainable. This might involve transparent governance structures, clear feedback mechanisms, or checks and balances to prevent abuses of power. Accountability is not a constraint but a tool for building trust and maintaining integrity. Consider the work of organizations like the NAACP or the Urban League, which integrate accountability into their advocacy efforts. Their success is built on trust earned through consistent action and adherence to their core values.

Investing in the next generation is a moral imperative for building a future rooted in trust. Mentorship plays a critical role in this process, providing young leaders with opportunities for growth, guidance, and collaboration. Mentorship is not simply about transferring knowledge—it is about fostering confidence, resilience, and the ability to innovate. Programs like My Brother's Keeper demonstrate how structured mentorship initiatives can transform communities by empowering young people to become agents of change. Trust, in this context, becomes the bridge that connects the wisdom of the past with the potential of the future, ensuring that the work we do today continues to thrive for generations to come.

These practical steps—cultivating self-trust, fostering collective action, creating systems of accountability, and mentoring the next generation—form the blueprint for transforming ideas into action. They remind us that progress is not an abstract concept but a lived practice, built on the foundation of trust and sustained through deliberate, collaborative efforts.

Conclusion: Trust in Action

The future is not something that happens to us—it is something we create. Every decision we make, every relationship we nurture, and every system we build is a deliberate act of creation. At the heart of this creation lies trust: the unseen force that connects individuals, strengthens communities, and sustains movements. Trust is not a passive ideal; it is an active practice—a foundation upon which a brighter, more connected world can be built.

Throughout this chapter, we have explored how trust translates into action, from mentoring the next generation to fostering collective responsibility and creating systems of accountability. Each of these steps highlights the transformative power of trust when it is applied with intention and integrity. Trust does not merely sustain progress; it fuels it, driving us to innovate, collaborate, and persevere in the face of challenges.

As we reflect on the themes woven throughout this book, it becomes clear that trust is not just a value to be admired—it is a skill to be cultivated. Trust is built every day, through deliberate actions, meaningful relationships, and courageous choices. It requires vulnerability, consistency, and a willingness to embrace both the risks and rewards of interdependence. In practicing trust, we create a legacy that will endure long after we are gone, shaping the world we leave for those who come after us.

Building a future rooted in trust is a collective endeavor, but it begins with each of us. It starts with self-trust—the confidence to align our actions with our values and to take bold steps toward progress. It extends outward, fostering connections that bridge divides and create communities grounded in mutual respect and shared purpose. It reaches into the systems and structures that govern our lives, ensuring that they reflect the principles of equity, accountability, and justice.

To move forward with trust in action, we must also embrace the lessons of the past. History teaches us that trust has always been the cornerstone of resilience and transformation. Whether in the movements for civil rights, the struggles for economic equity, or the quiet, daily acts of care and connection within families and communities, trust has been the thread that weaves individual efforts into collective progress. These lessons remind us that trust is both a gift and a responsibility—something to be earned, nurtured, and passed on.

Together, we have the power to create a world where trust is not the exception but the rule. A world where individuals, families, and communities thrive not despite adversity but because of the strength they draw from one another. A world where systems of power are held accountable, and every voice is valued. This is the future we envision—a future built on the unshakable foundation of trust. The work begins now, with each of us. It begins with the choices we make today, the relationships we invest in, and the systems we strive to improve. It requires clarity of purpose, unwavering commitment, and the courage to act even when the path forward is uncertain. Let us step into this work with determination, knowing that every action we take in the spirit of trust brings us closer to a future of connection, equity, and hope.

Trust in action is more than a practice; it is a promise—a promise to ourselves, to one another, and to the generations yet to come. It is the belief that our efforts today will ripple outward, creating a legacy that endures. Let us honor that promise by moving forward with clarity, purpose, and trust, building a future that reflects the very best of who we are and what we aspire to become. Together, we can ensure that the foundation we lay today becomes the bridge to a better tomorrow.

REFLECTION QUESTIONS

As we move forward, here are some questions to guide your journey toward building trust and fostering action.

How can you build trust within your personal relationships and broader community?

What actions can you take to mentor and empower the next generation?

How can collective action amplify your individual efforts toward creating systemic change?

Action Steps

To translate these principles into practice, consider the following steps as starting points.

Identify a community initiative to support through volunteerism or advocacy.

Mentor a young leader in your field or community, sharing your experiences and insights.

Advocate for policies that promote equity, accountability, and trust in your local government or organization.

Notes

Conclusion

Foundation For A Brighter Future

"We are each other's harvest; we are each other's business; we are each other's magnitude and bond."

— Gwendolyn Brooks

Trust is not merely a value; it is the guiding principle for building a brighter, more equitable future. Throughout this book, we have examined trust in its many dimensions: within ourselves, our families, our communities, and the systems that govern our lives. We have reflected on the importance of trusting the eyes behind us— the wisdom of our ancestors—and on the strength that comes from grounding our actions in spiritual and cultural foundations. Trust, at its essence, is the bridge that connects us to one another, to our history, and to the possibilities of tomorrow. It is a practice that calls us to elevate from our lower, reactive selves to our higher, purposeful selves, enabling us to create lasting change.

Legacy, woven throughout these reflections on trust, is not merely what we leave behind but what we actively build in the present. It is the stories we tell, the systems we create, and the values we pass on to future generations. For communities of African descent, legacy is a testament to resilience and cultural preservation—a continuation of an unbroken chain of wisdom passed down through generations. Yet legacy also demands action. It requires that we confront the challenges of our time with the same resolve and ingenuity that our ancestors demonstrated, ensuring the work of building a just world continues.

History teaches us that trust is not always easy. Integration, for example, offered hope for a more inclusive society but came at the cost of many Black institutions that had long served as pillars of strength and self-reliance. Schools, businesses, and networks central to the African American experience were often dismantled or undermined in the pursuit of broader inclusion. Despite these losses, trust endured—in the Black Church, in grassroots movements, and in individuals who refused to let injustice define their story. This resilience affirms trust as an active, transformative force, capable of turning even the most daunting challenges into opportunities for renewal.

The responsibility to build trust now falls on us. It is not enough to critique what is broken; we must also engage in the work of repair. Trust requires courage, vnerability, and a willingness to listen—especially to voices that have been historically marginalized or silenced. It challenges us to ask hard questions about our own roles within the systems we navigate: Are we building bridges or walls? Are we empowering others or seeking only to elevate ourselves? Are we living in alignment with the values we claim to uphold?

Trust is not a solitary endeavor but a collective one. It flourishes in relationships where accountability is mutual and respect is reciprocal. It grows in communities where leaders are transparent, actions align with values, and systems reflect fairness and equity. Trust is the foundation for creating institutions that sustain progress, ensuring every voice matters and every individual thrives. Whether through education, governance, or economic opportunity, the systems we build today will shape the lives of those who follow. This makes trust not only a moral imperative but also a practical necessity for sustainable change.

As we conclude, let us reflect on the journey we have shared through these pages. Let us carry forward the lessons and principles we have explored—trust as a daily practice, legacy as an active process, and service as the highest form of leadership. Trust is not a static achievement; it is a living, breathing practice that requires nurturing and growth. It is the thread that ties generations together, the force that transforms vision into action, and the foundation for a brighter, more connected world.

The future we seek is within our reach. It begins with small, deliberate acts: mentoring young leaders, listening to the wisdom of our elders, advocating for just policies, and building institutions that reflect our highest values. It is sustained by a collective commitment to equity and a belief in the transformative power of trust. And it is realized when we see trust not as an abstract ideal but as a way of life. Trust the journey. Trust the process. Trust the eyes behind you. In doing so, you are part of a larger story—a story of resilience, connection, and limitless possibility. Together, we can create a world where trust is not just a value but a guiding principle that shapes the legacies we leave and the futures we build.

Sources
Anna Julia Cooper, A Voice from the South
Dr. Maulana Karenga, Kwanzaa: A Celebration of Family, Community, and Culture
Dr. Marimba Ani, Let the Circle Be Unbroken
Howard Thurman, Meditations of the Heart
Septima Poinsette Clark, Echo in My Soul
Dr. Cheryl Tawede Grills, African-Centered Healing in Action
Dr. John Henrik Clarke, African World Revolution
Dr. Joy DeGruy, Post Traumatic Slave Syndrome
Dr. Claud Anderson, PowerNomics: The National Plan to Empower Black America
Michelle Alexander, The New Jim Crow: Mass Incarceration in the Age of Colorblindness
Angela Y. Davis, Are Prisons Obsolete?
Bryan Stevenson, Just Mercy: A Story of Justice and Redemption
Kimberlé Crenshaw, On Intersectionality: Essential Writings
Peter Block, Community: The Structure of Belonging
John C. Maxwell, The 5 Levels of Leadership: Proven Steps to Maximize Your Potential
Kwame Ture (Stokely Carmichael), Black Power: The Politics of Liberation
Kwame Nkrumah, Consciencism: Philosophy and Ideology for Decolonization
Nelson Mandela, Long Walk to Freedom
Dr. Molefi Kete Asante, Afrocentricity: The Theory of Social Change
Dr. Carter G. Woodson, The Mis-Education of the Negro
Dr. Joy DeGruy, Post Traumatic Slave Syndrome.
Dr. Claud Anderson, PowerNomics: The National Plan to Empower Black America.
Dr. Patricia Hill Collins, Black Feminist Thought: Knowledge, Consciousness, and the Politics of Empowerment.
Dr. Vincent Harding, There Is a River: The Black Struggle for Freedom in America.
Marimba Ani, Yurugu: An African-Centered Critique of European Cultural Thought and Behavior.
W.E.B. Du Bois, The Souls of Black Folk.
Dr. Asa G. Hilliard III, The Liberation of the African Mind.

Dr. Amos Wilson, The Developmental Psychology of the Black Child.
Dr. Chike Akua, Education for Transformation.
Dr. Cheryl Fields-Smith, "Black Homeschooling: Building Communities and Raising the Bar".
Malcolm X, The Autobiography of Malcolm X.
Ishakamusa Barashango, Revolutionary Wisdom: The Story of the City of Pali.

Sources

Chapter 1: The Self Revisited
Garvey, Marcus. Philosophy and Opinions.
Ani, Marimba. Yurugu: An African-Centered Critique of European Cultural Thought and Behavior.

Chapter 2: The Dynamics of Family Trust
African Proverbs on Family.

Chapter 3: Community Connectivity
Barashango, Ishakamusa. African People and European Holidays.
Collins, Patricia Hill. Black Feminist Thought: Knowledge, Consciousness, and the Politics of Empowerment.

Chapter 4: The Spiritual Dimensions of Trust
King Jr., Dr. Martin Luther. Strength to Love.
Ani, Marimba. Yurugu.

Chapter 5: Healing Generational Wounds
Hill Collins, Patricia. Black Feminist Thought.

Chapter 6: Igniting Minds: Education as the Bridge to Legacy
Du Bois, W.E.B. The Souls of Black Folk.
Fryer, Roland G. The Economics of Racial Discrimination.

Chapter 7: Leading with Purpose: Leadership Rooted in Trust
Collins, James. Good to Great.
Kouzes, James M., and Barry Z. Posner. The Leadership Challenge.

Chapter 8: Restoring Balance: Justice Rooted in Accountability
King, Dr. Martin Luther. Strength to Love.
Williams, Patricia J. The Alchemy of Race and Rights.

Chapter 9: Strength in Numbers: The Power of Unity and Action
Trotter, Joe W. The African American Experience in the Civil Rights Movement.
Obama, Barack. The Audacity of Hope.

Chapter 10: Trust and Justice
Obama, Barack. The Audacity of Hope.
King Jr., Dr. Martin Luther. Letter from Birmingham Jail.

Chapter 11: Trust and Shared Leadership
Burns, James MacGregor. Leadership.
West, Cornel. Race Matters.
Chapter 12: Creating Tomorrow: Legacy Through Trust
King Jr., Dr. Martin Luther. Strength to Love.
Washington, Booker T. Up from Slavery.
Chapter 13: Passing the Torch: Legacy as a Call to Action
Du Bois, W.E.B. The Souls of Black Folk.
Brooks, David. The Second Mountain.
Addendum for Chapter 10: Taking Local Action for Police Reform
Alexander, Michelle. The New Jim Crow.
Coates, Ta-Nehisi. Between the World and Me.
Addendum for Chapter 11: Building Local Leadership and Collaboration for Community Empowerment
Obama, Barack. The Audacity of Hope.
Booker, T.W. The Future of the American Negro.
Chapter 2 revised
Akbar, Na'im. Breaking the Chains of Psychological Slavery.
Ani, Marimba. Yurugu: An African-Centered Critique of European Cultural Thought and Behavior.
Collins, Patricia Hill. Black Feminist Thought: Knowledge, Consciousness, and the Politics of Empowerment.
DeGruy, Joy. Post Traumatic Slave Syndrome: America's Legacy of Enduring Injury and Healing.
Alexander, Michelle. The New Jim Crow: Mass Incarceration in the Age of Colorblindness.

Book Summary

"If You Can't Trust the Eyes Behind You: Reclaiming Narrative, Building Legacy, Empowering Communities" is a profound and urgent call to action, exploring trust as the foundation for healing, growth, and empowerment. Rooted in the stories, struggles, and triumphs of African-descended communities, this book redefines trust not as a passive belief but as a deliberate, transformative act that binds us to our ancestors, strengthens our present, and builds bridges to a thriving future.

Through an evocative blend of personal reflections, historical insights, and actionable strategies, the book takes readers on a journey to understand trust as the heartbeat of resilient families, empowered communities, and equitable systems. It challenges readers to reclaim stolen narratives, build institutions that honor cultural heritage, and instill a legacy of trust that inspires generations to come.

Themes and Structure
Organized into 13 compelling chapters, each section delves into a critical dimension of trust, weaving together storytelling, scholarship, and practical steps to ignite meaningful change. These chapters explore:
Trust in Ourselves: Overcoming internalized doubt to unlock personal growth and purpose.
Trust in Families: Rebuilding generational bonds to pass down wisdom, identity, and resilience.
Trust in Communities: Restoring fractured relationships and fostering collective empowerment.
Trust in Education: Liberating minds through culturally relevant teaching that honors history and prepares future leaders.
Trust in Justice: Demanding equity and accountability in systems that shape lives and futures.
Each chapter offers a blueprint for reclaiming trust as a tool for both survival and transformation, empowering readers to navigate life's complexities with clarity, purpose, and resolve.

A Spotlight on Legacy
One of the book's most transformative chapters, "Igniting Minds: Education as the Bridge to Legacy," examines education as the cornerstone of identity reclamation and liberation. Drawing on the works of visionaries like Dr. Asa Hilliard, Dr. Marimba Ani, Dr. Chike Akua and Dr. Amos Wilson, it illuminates how culturally anchored learning can dismantle systemic oppression while preparing the next generation to lead with knowledge, confidence, and cultural pride. The chapter bridges theory with personal narratives, offering readers tangible steps to make education a powerful tool for empowerment.

Purpose and Vision
This book is more than a collection of ideas—it is a clarion call to action. It equips readers with tools to:
Reclaim narratives erased by oppression and systemic inequities.
Strengthen familial and communal bonds to create enduring support systems.

Build institutions grounded in trust, cultural heritage, and shared values. Inspire future generations to lead with authenticity, courage, and purpose.

A Movement Toward Transformation
"If You Can't Trust the Eyes Behind You" is not just a book—it is a movement for reclamation, resilience, and empowerment. It challenges readers to reflect deeply on the power of trust in their own lives while providing a clear road map to restore, rebuild, and reimagine a world rooted in justice and equity. By reclaiming the wisdom of the past, acting intentionally in the present, and committing to the possibilities of the future, this book provides a guiding light for those ready to embrace the transformative power of trust.
This is more than a reading experience—it's an invitation to be part of a legacy in motion. Will you answer the call?

Alternative Book Summary:
In If You Can't Trust the Eyes Behind You: Reclaiming Narrative, Building Legacy, Empowering Communities, Kazemde Ajamu offers a profound exploration of trust—not just in others, but in ourselves. This powerful work redefines trust as an active, transformative force that is at the core of personal empowerment, healing, and social change. Drawing on the rich histories of African-descended communities and the wisdom of figures like Martin Luther King Jr., Malcolm X, Kwame Ture (Stokely Carmichael), and Kwame Nkrumah, Ajamu guides readers on a journey to reclaim their own narratives, strengthen relationships, and rebuild communities rooted in justice and equity.
At the heart of the book is the idea that trust begins within. The path to collective transformation starts with self-trust, where individuals are empowered to overcome internalized doubt and unlock their full potential. Ajamu argues that only when we trust ourselves can we begin to trust others, and from there, extend trust into our families, communities, and institutions.
With 13 compelling chapters, If You Can't Trust the Eyes Behind You takes readers through the multifaceted journey of reclaiming trust as a tool for survival and growth. The book covers vital topics such as:
Trust in Ourselves: Overcoming self-doubt and internalized oppres-

sion to embrace self-worth and purpose.

Trust in Families: Rebuilding generational ties to pass down wisdom, resilience, and cultural pride.

Trust in Communities: Restoring fractured relationships and fostering collective empowerment.

Trust in Education: Reclaiming education as a tool for liberation and leadership development.

Trust in Justice: Advocating for fair and equitable legal systems that serve all communities.

Ajamu builds on the legacies of those who fought for freedom and justice, emphasizing that true empowerment comes from understanding and reclaiming the trust that systemic oppression has attempted to erode. One of the book's most transformative chapters, "Igniting Minds: Education as the Bridge to Legacy," draws on the works of influential scholars like Dr. Asa Hilliard, Dr. Marimba Ani, and Dr. Chike Akua to explore how education can dismantle historical trauma and prepare future generations to lead with confidence and cultural pride.

Ultimately, If You Can't Trust the Eyes Behind You is a call to action for readers to take ownership of their own destinies and create change that transcends generations. With a road map for rebuilding trust from the individual to the collective, Ajamu offers hope and actionable steps for anyone seeking to empower themselves, their communities, and the world at large.

www.ingramcontent.com/pod-product-compliance
Lightning Source LLC
LaVergne TN
LVHW061546070526
838199LV00077B/6929